CW00421605

ENDORSEMENTS

Dan and Linda Wilson draw couples into a new realm of union that reflects the oneness believers will experience eternally with their Bridegroom, Jesus. Let your marriage be supernaturally transformed through the pages of this book by our covenant-keeping God. I highly recommend *7 Secrets of a Supernatural Marriage*.

DR. CHÉ AHN
Senior Pastor, HROCK Church, Pasadena, CA
President, Harvest International Ministry
International Chancellor, Wagner Leadership Institute

Healthy marriages and families are the backbone of a stable and prosperous nation. Today, more than ever, we need good, solid encouragement and instruction on how to enjoy a marriage that is like heaven on earth. Dr. Dan and Linda Wilson's book, *7 Secrets of a Supernatural Marriage*, will both refresh and empower your faith to lay hold of the fullness of all God has for you in marriage. No matter where you have walked or what you have gone through, there are keys contained in this book that will enable you to embrace new beginnings.

PATRICIA KING
Cofounder of XPmedia.com

In *7 Secrets of a Supernatural Marriage*, Dan and Linda Wilson have written a book that restores the elements of wonder and awe to marital relationships. The authors present a simple profile of a Christ-centered marriage in which love and honor are the paramount virtues, and the supernatural power of God is allowed to flow between the couple and God continually. I highly recommend this book not just to every married couple, but also to those who are getting married or want to get married!

JOAN HUNTER
Author/Evangelist, Joan Hunter Ministries

Dan and Linda Wilson brilliantly weave together the story of their supernatural encounters with God and how they have transformed both their lives and their marriage. In *7 Secrets of a Supernatural Marriage*, you will get an inside look into the process of how God opened Dan and Linda's hearts to receive this truth, the lessons they had to learn along the way—particularly that of lordship—and how living in God's supernatural presence has brought great benefits and blessings into their marriage. This is a timely and needed message for marriages in the church today. Once again, God chooses to touch every person in the body of Christ—the little ol' me's—with His presence and for His glory. Dan and Linda are certainly no exception.

RANDY CLARK
Founder and President, Global Awakening

The men of Issachar from 1 Chronicles 12:32 understood the times and knew what to do. In the times in which we are living today, the infrastructure of world society is deteriorating due to the onslaught of the enemy against covenant relationships in this hour. Dan and Linda Wilson's timely book, *7 Secrets of a Supernatural Marriage,* will inspire you to seek and find improved intimacy with your spouse by allowing the Holy Spirit to draw you together toward complete oneness in Him.

DR. ROBERT STEARNS
Executive Director, Eagles' Wings Ministries, Clarence, New York

7 Secrets is a treasure. In it, the Wilsons invite us to dream big, sharing the keys to spectacular marriage. Through childlike response to God's grace, these secrets lead to new heights of intimacy and fulfillment. They are not theoretical. Each secret manifests vividly in the beautiful romance Dan and Linda share with each other and the Lord. Having known them for over thirty years, I can testify that these two embody supernatural marriage and they glow with the joy and peace of Jesus. We would do well to follow their example!

PAUL LOONEY, M.D., PSYCHIATRIST AND PASTOR
Director, Hidden Manna Ministries
Author of *CrossTies: The Beatitudes for Every Believer*

What a story and testimony of a walk with God in marriage! This is what God intended when He created marriage for our good and welfare. As in all of life, we cannot live supernaturally without God in our affairs. We were not meant to love and live outside of God and His amazing grace. In a day when so many marriages are on the rocks, such a book is really needed to be able to appropriate the truths and the Truth that make such a marriage possible. Indeed a cord of three strands is the secret of such a time together! May our Lord revive holy marriage in our churches and homes.

PETER LORD
Pastor, Speaker, Author of *The 2959 Plan* and many more resources

Long before the Wilsons put pen to paper, those of us who have been blessed to know Dan and Linda have seen the unfolding of the concepts of this book. Their marriage has been godly, beautiful, and deep for decades. How incredible to see the transformation of a truly exemplary marriage into a supernatural marriage! The increased depth of oneness, passion, power, and joy in the Holy Spirit are invitingly presented in these pages.

BOB BEAVER
Pastor, Christian Church of San Angelo, San Angelo, Texas

I have had the privilege of knowing Dan and Linda Wilson for a number of years. Dan is a scientist and eye surgeon who looks for accuracy and knowledge founded on solid, tangible research. It is impressive that, at the same time, he recognizes the need for the miraculous work of God intervening in our lives and relationships. He and Linda pursue the heart of God with an intense focus, which is evident in *7 Secrets of a Supernatural Marriage*. I recommend this book to all who are married and all who intend to be married. I believe this material, if applied, can revolutionize marriages all across the world.

D. LELAND PARIS
President of Youth with a Mission, Tyler, Texas
Founder/CEO of Humanitarian Relief Organizations

Wow! When the Chinese in our churches first met Dan and Linda they were very surprised because, although grandparents, they appeared as a newlywed couple. They were one in spirit, heart, and mind as they daily walked as faithful Christians. I recommend this book for those who want to have the fullness of marriage that comes from being focused on the Lord. Anybody who wants to read this book will never, never be divorced.

"MISS CHOY"
Chinese leader of over 700 regional house church networks

We believe that marriage is honorable above all and is instituted by Almighty God. God always wants to see healthy marriages and united families come and worship Him in the church together. We really admire and thank Dr. Dan and Linda Wilson for their passion in writing *7 Secrets of a Supernatural Marriage*. Hundreds of broken families are already reunited in India through their teaching and books. We can boldly say that the divorce rate is now slow in our region of India just because of this couple. They are proven teachers and authors in India through their work and ministry. We cannot praise highly enough the vision and purpose of this book. We appreciate their emphasis on supernatural marriage. This is one of the best books on marriage written by a couple who practice what they preach. It's a book we urge every person to read and be blessed by. As they say, "Holy is always fun."

PASTOR IMANIYEL AND SIS NISSI JVOTHI VINNAKOTA
President and Vice President, Hope Mission, India

When Dan and Linda came to Kenya in May 2008, while in Mombasa, they taught wonderful lessons on marriage. These teachings removed walls satan had erected against our marriages and satanic limits came off. It was like the children of Israel during the time of Gideon (Judges 7:16–21). These teachings taught by Dan and Linda will cause the glory of God to be seen in our marriages just like when the jars were broken and the torches shined brightly.

BRYSON AND NELLY NYONGESA
Church Leaders, Kenya

SEVEN7SECRETS

OF A SUPERNATURAL MARRIAGE

THE
JOY OF
SPIRIT-LED
INTIMACY

DR. DAN & LINDA WILSON

BroadStreet Publishing
Racine, Wisconsin, USA
www.broadstreetpublishing.com

7 Secrets of a Supernatural Marriage: The Joy of Spirit-Led Intimacy

Some of the content of *7 Secrets of a Supernatural Marriage* has been adapted
from *Supernatural Marriage* published by XP Publishing.

© 2014 Dr. Dan and Linda Wilson

ISBN-13: 978-1-4245-4944-3 (print book)
ISBN-13: 978-1-4245-4948-1 (ebook)

Cover design by Garborg Design Works, Inc. | www.garborgdesign.com
Interior design/typesetting by Katherine Lloyd | www.theDESKonline.com

*Stock or custom editions of BroadStreet Publishing titles may be purchased in
bulk for educational, business, ministry, fundraising, or sales promotional use.
For information, please e-mail info@broadstreetpublishing.com.*

Printed in China

To Bob and Rachel Beaver,
Tony and Barb Huston,
and Scott and Rissa Marlar.

Thanks for inspiring us with your
supernatural marriages!
We really love and honor you!

ACKNOWLEDGEMENTS

We are eternally grateful to our astounding God. He blesses us at every turn. We are His!

Our hearts are full of thanksgiving to all who have stood with us in our marriage and in the writing of this book. Rissa and our awesome intercessory team, we could not have done it without you. Kris Vallotton, we honor you for your strong stance for purity and your dedication to vibrant marriages. Thank you for writing the foreword for us in the midst of your busy schedule! Bless you, brother.

Patricia King, you were the first to embrace the concept of Supernatural Marriage. Thank you for daring us to dream big! Carol Martinez, you have carried us through step by step and have become a dear friend in the process. Ryan Adair, thanks for your input and grace. And David Sluka, you are a delight! Thanks for all your cheerleading and expertise.

Paul Looney and Bob Beaver, you godly men have been instrumental in our spiritual formation. Thank you for walking with us!

It is our heartfelt prayer that marriages all around the globe will be *supernatural,* shining the light of Jesus and the joy of the

Lord for all the world to see. *Now to the King eternal, immortal, invisible, the only God, be honor and glory for ever and ever. Amen* (1 Timothy 1:17).

Dan & Linda

CONTENTS

FOREWORD

Dan and Linda Wilson's new book, *7 Secrets of a Supernatural Marriage*, will wake you into new dimensions of passion, covenant, and romance with your spouse. It will shift the very foundation of what it means to come into agreement with the kingdom of heaven for your marriage. This book is full of insight and godly wisdom, and it will challenge, inspire, and equip you to change the way you view intimacy.

The Wilsons exhort their readers to walk in their divine decree as world changers and history makers through supernatural marriage. *7 Secrets of a Supernatural Marriage* is a Messiah's mandate...a divine strategy to raise up powerful and fulfilled marriages filled with extravagant intimacy and continual communion.

Imagine a world where every marriage is supernatural—where every husband and wife have embraced who they truly are and are living from their identity. There would be no broken homes. Orphanages would be closed down. Children's hearts would turn to their fathers. There would be no sexual addictions, no desire for pornography. Divorce would not exist.

Supernatural marriages are a sign and a wonder that will lead the world into revival.

Whether you are newlywed, have been married for years, or are preparing for a great marriage, *7 Secrets of a Supernatural Marriage* will equip you to fulfill your dreams and could change the future of your marriage. No matter what your marriage currently looks like, this book will take you to the next level. I highly recommend it!

KRIS VALLOTTON
Senior Associate Leader, Bethel Church, Redding, CA
Cofounder of Bethel School of Supernatural Ministry
Author of ten books, including *The Supernatural Ways
of Royalty* and *Spirit Wars*

PUTTING SUPER
INTO YOUR NATURAL

Every Sleeping Beauty wants the man of her dreams to kiss her,
awakening her to a marriage where they live happily ever after.
Supernatural marriage is not a fairy tale. You can know the se-
crets so that you can enjoy the ultimate marriage experience with
your mate.

Did you have childhood fantasies? It is likely that during childhood you had dreams of what it would be like to someday be married—perhaps even pretending to go through marriage ceremonies in play with your friends. God placed those thoughts of marriage in your heart.

During your time of engagement, there was probably a gradually increasing anticipation and excitement about the upcoming wedding—the two of you being united to become one. The optimistic hope you held about how wonderful marriage could be was not vain. It was based in the reality of God's desire for you and your partner.

Do you want your marriage to be *super*? Of course you

do. Everyone hopes their love relationship will be above and beyond the norms for society. Who wouldn't want experiences with their partner in marriage to be satisfying and good?

You wanted and still want your marriage to be like heaven on earth. So does God. The astounding kind of marriage you desire is an experiential reality within your grasp. Supernatural marriage is not a fairytale, but to reach it you must be willing to enter the *supernatural* realm of God.

Now, let's go up to an even higher level. Think far beyond what you have expected in the past. Kick it up a notch. Allow your mind to freely consider the possibilities for marriage that are beyond what you have ever asked for or imagined (Ephesians 3:20). Dream of having a marriage described by you and others with these words: *phenomenal, astonishing, astounding.*

This is the kind of relationship you desire deep in your heart. It is far beyond the norm, surpassing even the level we would describe as super. But you will never enjoy the ultimate experiences available in marriage if your relationship is limited to the natural realm. You and your partner were created for the highest level of marriage available on earth: *Supernatural Marriage.*

By this point you might be asking, "What exactly do you mean by the word *supernatural*?" We are very pleased to answer this question. But before we go there, let's begin by discussing the meaning of the opposite word, *natural*.

Nature can be defined as the external, observable, measurable universe that surrounds us. It is thought to exist within the constraints of time. We are continually and keenly aware of the natural realm, making it easy to discuss and understand. The truth is that reality extends far beyond the things we perceive in the natural.

Something that is supernatural is not in conformity to the ordinary course of nature. It departs from what is usual and normal, and often is unable to be explained by science or the laws of nature.

In western culture it is common to fully believe things observed in the natural realm while questioning and excluding all things supernatural. But, as children of God, participation in the supernatural realm can and should be our normal experience. Our God is a supernatural being and we relate to Him in His realm of the Spirit. We can only receive His spiritual gifts and blessings as our marriages participate in the supernatural. Though we cannot fully comprehend the things of God, it is vital that each of us trusts in the LORD with all of our heart and lean not on our own understanding (see Proverbs 3:5). This is an exciting mystery.

We read in the Bible that flesh and blood cannot inherit the kingdom of God, nor does the perishable inherit the imperishable (1 Corinthians 15:50). One day the perishable things of the natural will no longer exist. The supernatural realm transcends time and will exist forever. This is the proper realm of focus for both our lives and our marriages. A supernatural marriage is deeply rooted in eternity.

Our God is Spirit (John 4:24). Husbands and wives are also spirit-beings. We worship and relate to Him spirit-to-Spirit in the eternal, supernatural realm. He longs for you and your marriage to join Him there. When you open your heart and mind to this realm, you obtain access to everything that is needed for an astounding marriage, such as:

- Intimacy with God
- Wisdom
- Understanding
- Council
- Power
- Knowledge
- Fear of the Lord
- Heavenly encounters
- Spiritual dreams
- Fruit of the Spirit

When the supernatural invades the natural realm, the result is always miraculous. The miracle of salvation awaits those who are lost. The sick have the opportunity to receive the blessing of miraculous healing. Likewise, spouses involved in any type of marital relationship can have their lives transformed through the miracle of supernatural marriage. Yes, *your* marriage can be catapulted to new levels of intimacy, joy, and productivity through connection with God in His supernatural realm. With man this is impossible, but with God all things are possible (Matthew 19:26).

The Treasure of Supernatural Marriage

Supernatural marriage is the intended destiny of every marriage established within the kingdom of God—a lofty goal consistent with the glory of heaven! No marital relationship is perfect, yet too often we settle for seeking and barely reaching mediocre goals in marriage. This book sets the standard for marriage extremely high—not to discourage anyone but to stimulate everyone to pursue and experience the wonders only available to marital partners who function within the supernatural realm.

Supernatural marriage is filled with the presence, passion, and power of God. The glory of the Lord is constantly present and readily available to those who seek Him. When His glory invades the union of a man and woman in marriage, the result is miraculous transformation of each of them individually and as a couple.

God's plan for marriage is amazing and amazingly good! When you and your mate are filled with the glorious presence of God's Spirit, you are enabled to function with supernatural wisdom, understanding, and authority. Your marriage and ministry exit the restraints of the natural world, allowing you to do wonderful things that can only be accomplished through the counsel and might of God. The two of you change the world and advance His kingdom. You also bring great honor to the King of kings and Lord of lords.

What about Me?

You may be thinking as you read this chapter, "Where is my supernatural marriage? What happened to the 'happily ever after' I dreamed of before our marriage?" You feel assaulted, and rightly so! You and your mate have been attacked by satan himself, the "thief" who comes to steal and kill and destroy (John 10:10). Satan hates supernatural marriage and is intent upon stealing every one of the astonishing things God planned for husbands and wives to enjoy.

Hope will be rekindled by the second half of John 10:10, where Jesus promises all believers, "I have come that they may have *life*, and have it to the full" (emphasis added). The Greek word from the original Bible is *zoe*—translated into English as "life." *Zoe* means "absolute fullness of life." If you are a believer, this promise is for you. God wants your marriage to be absolutely full of abundant, joy-filled life. You can be a man or woman fully alive!

Regardless of your yesterdays, tomorrow begins as a brand-new day. God is not limited by your disappointments in life. His plans for you remain good and His promises will not fail.

As encouragement to you, let's look at the plight of the Israelites as they were trapped between the Egyptian army and the Red Sea (Exodus 13 and 14). As with your marriage, satan was also intent on destroying their destiny.

The children of Israel had faced many challenges in the past. Their painful memories were based on experiences that were real—slavery, oppression, frequent abuse. When they reached the shores of the Red Sea, they all realized their escape route from Egypt was blocked. Thousands of chariots and soldiers were approaching from behind. Every man, woman, and child could see and hear Pharaoh's army coming. They were trapped. In the natural realm there was no way of escape.

But the God of Israel lived, and He lives in the supernatural realm. The miraculous trumped the expected as the power of God made a path for them through the sea. God's glory led them across dry ground toward the land He had promised to His people.

The God of Israel is also our God. He is no less miraculous today. He is willing and able to bless you far beyond your expectations. Are you ready to be led into the promised land of supernatural marriage?

God's love for you as His child is no less than what He had for the children of Israel.

His plans for you are just as good. His promises remain unfailing. You can trust our Father with every part of your life—including your marriage.

The Israelites followed a cloud by day and a pillar of fire by night, both filled with the glory of God. In supernatural marriage you are led and protected by this same glory. The Spirit of God is literally in husband and wife as they live, loving and serving Him together. There are no limitations in the supernatural realm of God.

With the Spirit of God in the center of your marriage, two will be bonded together forever as one. Intimacy between husband and wife will be enhanced as intimacy with God grows rich and deep. Your marriage will be transformed to be fully pleasing to Him. Each of you will be pleased as well.

What Will it Look Like?

At this point you might be saying to yourself, "This all sounds good in theory, but what does this kind of a marriage look like?" We are delighted that you asked. It will be our pleasure to respond.

Love together. The way a supernatural spouse treats his or her partner clearly demonstrates true *agape* love. This is not an act. Loving one another becomes as natural as breathing. The Bible declares that "God is love" (1 John 4:8). His transforming love continually flows into them by the Spirit and is joyfully shared between them. Love becomes a recognizable constant in their relationship.

Worship together. Supernatural husbands and wives place a high priority on spending time together in worship. It is valuable to worship God regularly in the corporate setting of a church. But some of our most special memories have been when we chose to sing and dance before Him in the privacy of our own home—proclaiming the glory of the one who made us one. We believe this brings a big smile to Jesus' face. Have you tried this yet? We think you will like it!

Pray together. Prayer is the place of deepening relational intimacy with God. Supernatural couples join together to hear the voice of their loving Father and share with Him the most intimate of thoughts. Not surprisingly, their marital love relationship grows stronger and deeper as together they draw closer to God through prayer. This becomes a delightful time that encourages true vulnerability before *Abba* and each other.

Minister together. Supernatural husbands and wives are empowered by the Spirit. As was Jesus, they too are anointed to preach good news to the poor, proclaim freedom for the prisoners and recovery of sight for the blind, to release the oppressed, to proclaim the year of the Lord's favor (Luke 4:18–19). In ministry together they find that two really are better than one. It's the third strand of the Holy Spirit that completes the effective team (Ecclesiastes 4:9–12).

Dream together. It is said that a picture is worth a thousand words. The value of the simplest dream from God is without measure. As we pray together each night before going to sleep, we ask for dreams from heaven that would help us understand the thoughts and plans of our Father. Supernatural spouses share their dreams with each other. Each can receive interpretation of dreams that help them to be understood. They work together to apply each message from God to their work in the kingdom. As we read in the Bible, dreams can be powerfully effective when understood and used well.

Read together. Even a few verses of Scripture read together will unite your spirits. One of you will see something important the other might have missed. Discussing the thoughts will help cement them in your hearts and minds. Personally, we enjoy reading together at bedtime. You might prefer this sweet time over your morning coffee.

Hope together. Marriage is not without its challenging times. Jesus warns us, "In this world you will have trouble" (John 16:33). At times we may become discouraged. Husbands and wives can safely hold on to the promise from the second half of this famous verse, where Jesus proclaims, "But take heart! I have overcome the world."

Supernatural partners in marriage encourage each other to hold on to true hope. They have an expectation, even a knowing that every obstacle in their lives can and will be overcome. The source of this hope is not each other, but their Father in heaven who joined them together. We are reminded in Scripture that "hope does not disappoint us, because God has poured out his love into our hearts by the Holy Spirit, whom he has given us" (Romans 5:5). When we, by the Spirit, receive the perfect love of the Father, hope becomes a present reality that can never be taken away.

The Key to the Seven Secrets

We are dreamers who value the times God speaks to us in the night. Dan received two dreams that have led us into the kind of ministry we do and have helped us explain to others the revelation of supernatural marriage.

In the first dream, the hand of God placed a special key into Dan's hand, the perfect key for opening a treasure chest. In the second dream, God was playing a simple childhood game in the sand with Dan. The second dream gave us further understanding of the first. Combining the interpretation of the two dreams: *Childlikeness is the key to the treasure of supernatural marriage.*

Why would God want us to be like children?

In an ideal world childhood is pretty great! The child's job description is "play." His responsibility is simple: obey Mommy and Daddy. Food is prepared for him. Clothes are provided for her. They are taken everywhere they need to go. Everything they need and even most of what they desire is there for them. Safety is ensured. Daydreaming is encouraged.

Wonder and awe accompany the child everywhere he goes.

She is innocent, pure, naïve to the things of the world. He is free in expressing emotion and passionate about everything. She is compassionate and is also quick to forgive. He loves to laugh. Who wouldn't want to return to this childhood bliss?

Jesus said, "I tell you the truth, anyone who will not receive the kingdom of God like a little child will never enter it" (Luke 18:17). God wants us to respond to Him in the same way the children described above live. He wants to nurture us, to provide for us, to direct us. Wow! The responsibility is off our shoulders! His yoke, Jesus said, is easy (see Matthew 11:30).

God's supernatural kingdom is full of wonder and awe. As His dearly loved child, you get to delight in it! This kingdom is filled with peace that is not available in the natural realm of our world. He desires your marriage to be no less remarkable than the rest of your journey with Him. But to enter the realm of kingdom blessing you must be willing to receive what God has planned for you as His little child. Are you ready?

Those who are older often look down on children because of their naïveté. Certainly there is a downside to being too easily influenced by others. But a good attribute of those who are naïve is that they are teachable. God is pleased when we are childlike enough that we realize there is still much to learn.

Children are adept at giving and receiving love. *Abba* is a Greek name in the Bible for our Father in heaven (Romans 8:15). The English equivalent of this informal word would be Daddy. He is our wonderful daddy who loves us and wants to take care of us every day. There is nothing to fear from His perfect love. As His children we can absolutely trust our Abba.

There is much we can learn from the simple life of an obedient child. The plan is the same every day. Listen to Daddy and do what He asks. He has known us since long before we were born (Jeremiah 1:5). Daddy knows best. Like Jesus, our ideal response is to listen to Him through the Spirit and immediately obey.

And remember the child's job description: play. What could be more fun than playing as a little child under the shelter of our Abba's wings? We get to play being married each and every day, taking hold of the abundant life He promised!

Childlikeness is the key that opens the treasure chest. Inside the chest you will discover its treasure: the *7 Secrets of a Supernatural Marriage*. In the following chapters you will be given access to each.

7 Secrets Suggestion

As marriage missionaries we get to travel to the nations. While on ministry trips we try to keep our eyes open for carnivals with Ferris wheels and playgrounds that have seesaws. Holy is fun! In Mongolia we had a blast taking a pastor couple and their kids to an amusement park. What fun to ride a Ferris wheel in Ulaanbaatar! And we will share a little secret with you. We make it a priority to *play* in every country we visit.

Think of a childlike activity you could enjoy doing together—something that is not expensive and that is light-hearted. Get in the habit of doing it! Constantly be on the lookout for opportunities to play.

SECRET 1: LORDSHIP

To enter the astonishing realm of supernatural marriage, we must experience a paradigm shift: Jesus is not only Savior, He is Lord. Embracing this reality is the essential first step toward enjoying the love experiences we all desire and need.

Does it surprise you that the first secret to a supernatural marriage is lordship? This word is something many don't want to think about, much less act upon. It sounds like sheer drudgery. Believe us when we tell you that lordship is not a prison meant to restrain you. It is a secret that will release you to enjoy freedom beyond what you have ever imagined.

In all honesty, we had some apprehension about tackling the subject of lordship so early in this book. After we prayed about this for weeks, God revealed to us that it is the essential first step toward the other six secrets of supernatural marriage.

As is true of all seven, we gain access to understanding the secret of lordship using the key of childlikeness.

Remember the lazy days of summer as a child when you

were free from schedules, school, and homework? It was a time filled with a delightful lack of responsibility. During summer vacation from elementary school, you could play with friends, running and laughing as the hours passed by uncounted. Oh, to be like that child again!

As an adult you delight in breaks from the pressures of being in charge. Date nights are wonderful, vacations prized. These times of pure liberty are cherished but few. Late in the night you lie in bed sleepless, wishing someone else could make all the big decisions. Wouldn't it be great to not be the responsible one anymore?

Recognizing that God is in control places responsibility in its proper position. Your loving Daddy *is* in charge, and you can fully trust Him. As His child your role is to allow Abba to make all the decisions. Simply do what He asks. His plans are always good.

With Jesus as Lord of your life, you will be brought into the glorious freedom of the children of God (Romans 8:21). When He is also Lord for your mate, your relationship will grow in ways you cannot imagine. A marriage committed to satisfying the desires of God will be blessed beyond measure. This is the legacy lordship affords.

The ABCs of Lordship

Let's think about lordship using the simple analogy of the ABCs. Jesus walked on the earth completely in the Z zone of lordship. Through His life of obedience Jesus joyfully accomplished everything the Father asked Him to do. With Christ in us we can also complete our portion of God's glorious plan (Colossians 1:27).

Initially, as His dearly loved children, we begin walking in lordship in the early stage of "A, B, C." When we start getting comfortable with this, He has the audacity to ratchet it up a notch! So we learn how to listen to Him more attentively, and we discover that it is easy to obey. Soon God sees that we are secure in "D, E, and F," and He advances us yet again. When our commitment to lordship is real, God is pleased to lead us into its highest levels.

Surprisingly, the ever-increasing demands of lordship are easy! As our hearts beat more and more in sync with heaven's, we discover that His ways truly are better than ours. It is pleasurable to partner with Him. Sometimes we squirm, as our wills want to be boss. But when we say yes to God, it is always for our good. He knows exactly how much we can handle. The Holy Spirit stretches us *for* us—to bless us and prosper us.

To give an example of what this lordship journey looks like, Dr. Dan will share part of his story.

Dan's Story

All my life I felt intensely drawn toward marriage—even when I was a small child. God placed this desire for marriage in me for His purposes, to be used for His glory. For years I misunderstood and misapplied this yearning, seeking to satisfy its intention in the natural realm through my own perceptions and abilities. The sins of selfishness, stubbornness, and compromise were prominent in my life.

In spite of my failings, God did not revoke His special plan for my marriage. My Father loves me and loves marriage with all His heart. However, He did not satisfy this deep desire of my heart until I had accepted Jesus' lordship over my life.

God said through Isaiah thousands of years before, "I will give you the treasures of darkness, riches stored in secret places, so that you may know that I am the LORD, the God of Israel, who summons you by name" (45:3). Unknown to me at the time, my desire for an outstanding marriage was meant to draw me into a supernatural marriage. This treasure was hidden in a secret place. God wanted it discovered and released to me and to the one who would become my wife. But the marriage I craved would never be obtainable in the natural realm alone. The treasure of supernatural marriage was hidden by darkness until it was made visible by the glorious light from God's supernatural realm.

When I was eleven years old, a wonderful camp counselor asked if I was ready to accept Jesus as my Lord and Savior. I said, "Yes!" But I had no clue what true lordship really meant. I just assumed that, with a little effort, lordship would follow after salvation. To my surprise, it did not. My plan became to make Jesus 95 percent Lord and gradually work on the remainder over time.

I foolishly allowed years to pass through high school, college, and most of medical school before being willing to make a 100 percent commitment. I now describe that time of life as "the years the locusts have eaten" (Joel 2:25). I knew Jesus was not Lord of certain areas of my life, but I stubbornly put off submission to Him in those areas. It was similar to what I heard Juan Carlos Ortiz say on one occasion that we often sing with our voices the hymn "He Is Lord," while whispering in our minds, "But I am the prime minister." My self-satisfaction and acceptance of partial obedience led to much pain and injury, both to myself and others. The enemy had deceived me into settling for only a small part of the glory God made completely available to His children. For a time, I allowed goals and pleasures in the natural realm to take priority over the divine plans and commands of the God who created nature.

I saw holiness as a burden placed on us by a God who expected a little too much of us. I tried in my own strength to honor God in many ways, but intentionally held on to sin by being selfish, impure, and stubbornly resistant to the changes He required. The basic problem underlying my disobedience was that my love for God was very weak. I was not even close to understanding His beautiful supernatural love for me.

In the final year of medical school, my two most pressing goals were to become a doctor and to find a godly wife. Both of these goals were good in and of themselves, but the problem was the way I pursued them. My life was out of balance. I spent so much time and effort trying to find a woman to love, I hardly paid any attention to developing a love relationship with God, the eternal source of all true love. As I strived on my own to find fulfillment, my dearest relationships crumbled all around me.

Outwardly my life looked like a glorious success story, but

inside it was obvious I was headed for complete failure. I knew the glory of the Lord was not in me. I was badly missing the goal God had placed before me. My incomplete acceptance of Jesus' lordship had dragged me downward for years, yet God was prepared to forever change me in a moment.

One afternoon I fell on my face before God in complete despair. With sincerity I declared that I was incapable of being in charge of my life. I released control to Jesus and declared Him to be Lord of all. I really had no idea what that meant or what it would look like in day-to-day life. How would this all play out? What exactly does one do when Jesus is Lord? I didn't know what to expect in the future. The important thing was that for the first time I trusted God to lead me into that future. He began to teach me how to live and how to love.

Two weeks later my long struggle to find the woman I should marry surprisingly and miraculously ended in the medical school library. I was purposefully searching through the library for a misplaced magazine in which I could read about an upcoming event in Houston, hoping I could convince someone to go on a date with me. Unknowingly, I was on a God-ordained mission, unaware of how successful the mission would be.

Shockingly, suddenly, and unexpectedly, my search for a godly wife came to an end. I believe I was divinely led to the audio/visual department, a rather strange place to look for a magazine. The woman working at the counter had a kind smile, a sparkle in her eye, and an aura about her that made it clear she was a child of the King. I could sense the glory of the Lord in Linda, and I liked it! God made us both immediately aware that something astounding had happened. It was the most joyful moment in my then twenty-five years of life.

Just as happened in my decision to declare Jesus as Lord, God had ordained something of profound significance to happen in the briefest of moments. In the natural realm our meeting seemed random and unplanned, but I am confident the Holy Spirit choreographed the entire event. It was God's unpredictable but perfect plan, enacted at exactly the right moment, that supernaturally brought the two of us together to become one.

God places within each of us a lifelong desire to receive and give love. His plan is that we would receive His perfect love, return that love to Him, and share it with all whom we encounter. This is precisely what we do in supernatural marriage. God continually pours His love into the hearts of husband and wife by the Holy Spirit. Almost without effort they share this love with each other as they live together day by day. God's love changes them and strengthens their marriage. Then, with joy, they return it to Him through praise.

Holy love flowing through us drastically alters how we think and act. It literally transforms us, changing who we are and who we will become. This pure and effective form of love cannot be produced by effort in the natural realm. It cannot be manufactured from within our own minds or hearts. Holy love can only be received as a gift from God, who supernaturally places it in our hearts.

Lordship: Complete Obedience Motivated by Love

The supernatural gift of love we receive from God has two main purposes.

The first is that it enables us to fully and freely love one another. When we love others, it completes His love in us. What a grand opportunity to participate in this beautiful and eternal circle of love!

As partners in marriage receiving God's supernatural love, we are empowered to love each other deeply and consistently. The purpose of this love relationship is much bigger than the marriage itself. Its ultimate destiny is to complete the circle, which begins and ends within God's everlasting love. John writes, "No one has ever seen God; but if we love one another, God lives in us and his love is made complete in us" (1 John 4:12). One of the ways God's love is revealed in the earth today is through husbands and wives being submitted to His lordship and letting His love be expressed through their marriage relationship. Even though no one has seen God, people see Him in a sense via His love manifested in us.

The second purpose of God's gift of perfect love is to make true obedience possible. Jesus said, "If anyone loves me, he will obey my teaching. My Father will love him, and we will come to him and make our home with him" (John 14:23). Obedience is the expected result of the holy Lover taking up residence within the wholly loved. God's plans for our lives are astonishingly good and He wants to prosper us, providing hope and a future (Jeremiah 29:11). His design is that we experience joy and deep satisfaction in our relationships with others, particularly in marriage. However, God's planned destiny for holy matrimony will not be realized until His perfect love dwells within each marital partner, enabling them not only to truly love each other but also to walk in authentic obedience.

Through our obedience, the eternal, self-perpetuating flow of God's love can be seen. We receive His perfect gift of love and it supernaturally leads us to accept and respond to Him as Lord. Our greatest joy becomes obeying God, because we desire to please Him. He becomes our dearest friend who restores our souls and guides us "in paths of righteousness for his name's sake" (Psalm 23:3). Joyfully obedient, we remain in His love, for His love has been made complete. "But if anyone obeys his word, God's love is truly made complete in him" (1 John 2:5). This cycle of love and obedience has a beginning but no intended end. *God's desire is that we remain both in love with Him and obedient to Him forever.*

"God is love" (1 John 4:8), and He is full of glory (Habakkuk 3:3). When we receive God's holy love, we are transformed to become more like Him, empowering us to love without restraint and obey without hesitation. As we reflect the Lord's glory, His glory is forever increased. What a joy to participate in this eternal cycle of love and obedience! Paul writes, "And we, who with unveiled faces all reflect the Lord's glory, are being transformed into his likeness with ever-increasing glory, which comes from the Lord, who is the Spirit" (2 Corinthians 3:18).

True obedience seems far off and unobtainable when we

think of it with our natural minds. But as we gaze into the loving eyes of the Father, obeying all His desires becomes normal, instinctive, and effortless. Remember, Jesus says His yoke is easy. An intimate love relationship with the Father through Jesus is what makes the burden of obedience light. But we cannot fully receive God's love, individually or in a marriage, until we make the decision to pursue complete obedience, making Jesus *truly* Lord of our lives.

This was the stumbling block during my teen years and early twenties: I knew God desired that I fully follow His ways, yet I deliberately pursued the course of incomplete obedience. The patience of God allows for our imperfection, but His justice requires change in those who are knowingly disobedient. We may describe our rebellion as naughtiness or admit to others that we sometimes "slip up" or succumb to an occasional indiscretion. These euphemisms may appease our consciences, but they do nothing to limit the destructive effects of willful sin in our lives and in our marriages.

Lordship: The Pathway to Intimacy

Isaiah prophesied that Jesus would have "the Spirit of knowledge and of the fear of the LORD" (11:2). In this passage, the Spirit of knowledge is linked to the fear of the Lord. The Spirit of knowledge allowed Jesus, and it allows us, to intimately know and appreciate God. If we know God, we will love Him.

When we receive the fear of the Lord, God deposits within our souls the insatiable desire to respond to Him with complete obedience. This kind of intimate knowing of God is essential if we are to develop rich intimacy in marriage. Through divine relationship God imparts to us His perfect love, leading us into obedience and miraculously transforming us into the mature spouses, parents, and lovers He intended us to be.

To know God is to love Him. What is there not to love in our God? Abba is the perfect daddy. He is sweet. He is tender. He is kind. He is patient. He adores you! And He adores your spouse. Daddy wants marriage to exceed your expectations—to knock your socks off! It is a joy to serve Him forever.

Did your dad ever try to coax you into jumping into a pool with him? That took a lot of courage and required that you trust your father completely. But after the initial jump you wanted to do it again and again, right? Leaping into the supernatural love of God is just the same. You know He is trustworthy. After you work up the courage to jump in, you will want to do it again and again. Life in the "pool" with God is exhilarating! He will catch you every time. As you allow Him to be Lord, you will find this to be the safest and most wonderful life you can lead.

Revert to being like a child who is content to allow another to make the decisions. Let God be in control of your heart, mind, and will. Give him your emotions and imagination as well. Anything you hold back increases your responsibility. Trust God to control every part of your life and marriage. You will find rest when He is Lord (Jeremiah 6:16).

We began our discussion of lordship using the simple analogy of the ABCs. We all want to be near the end of the alphabet the next day after we proclaim that Jesus is Lord. The truth is that it takes time and transformation for our level of obedience to be consistent with the declaration we made. If your commitment is real, do not be discouraged when your actions show you have not yet reached Z. God knows your heart. He who began a good work in you will carry it on to completion (Philippians 1:6).

Ultimately, lordship is an individual decision and not one made by a married couple. But there is nothing that will bless your marriage more than you making this commitment to God. When both you and your partner join together in this pledge, watch out! Be prepared to experience astonishing things together with Jesus as Lord.

Supernatural Marriage in the Nations

Lordship. We often hear of couples where one spouse is a strong Christian but the other is not. This was the case with our good friends Bishop Samson and Mary Merlin of India. Mary Merlin was a devoted believer in Jesus. She fully understood lordship and was totally committed to Jesus as Lord. Often at night Samson would awaken to find that she was not in bed—she was kneeling in prayer. This infuriated him to the point that he would berate her, threaten her, and occasionally even beat her. Each time she would smile at him in the midst of her pain and say to him, "Jesus loves you."

One day at work, Samson was in a horrible accident. A big pressure tank exploded, killing one man and sending Samson to the hospital with serious injuries. The physicians were sure that his leg would need to be amputated. An unknown visitor dropped by his room and left a book on the nightstand. That evening Samson was in tremendous pain. Even with pain medicine and a sleeping pill, he was sleepless. His nurse suggested that he try reading.

The only book available was the one on the nightstand: a Bible. Samson opened the book and began reading where it fell open. These words seemed to jump off the page: "Blessed are the pure in heart, for they shall see God" (Matthew 5:8). He could hardly contain his excitement. He had always wanted to see God!

The words touched Samson; he cried and cried. The nurse told him that he was crying because Jesus was touching him. She told him to pray. "I do not know how to pray to this God" was his response. She told him that simply saying "Jesus" was enough. He closed his eyes while repeatedly saying, "Jesus," again and again until he drifted into sleep.

While he was sleeping, a bright light appeared. This light came nearer and nearer until it touched him. Samson then saw the hand of God write in neon letters, "RESIGN. COME. I NEED YOU."

The following morning he was remembering this vivid dream when instantly he received a vision of God's hand again writing the same words: "RESIGN. COME. I NEED YOU."

When Mary Merlin arrived to see him, he immediately told her that he must resign his stable job and go to Bible school.

He had given his heart and life to Jesus, acknowledging Him as both Savior and Lord. She simply looked him in the eye and said, "I know." What a woman!

Today Bishop Samson and Mary Merlin oversee more than 3,500 churches around the world. They have pastor training schools and orphanages under their supervision. He has traveled to more than 110 nations with the gospel. And, as will come as no surprise, his leg is healthy and strong. With the declaration that Jesus is Lord, Samson was saved, his leg was healed, and their marriage entered the supernatural realm of God.

7 Secrets Suggestion

Our friend Mary Merlin was committed to Jesus as her Lord long before her husband came along. Is there an aspect of your life or your marriage that has yet to be fully entrusted to Jesus? Now is a great time to make that commitment. Declare that Jesus is Lord over that. Yes, even that! Praise Him that He has you and your mate in His strong, capable hand.

SECRET 2: PASSION

We all want to be red-hot lovers. This requires passion. Your heart beating in sync with God's opens the door for you to wholeheartedly love both God and your mate simultaneously.

Passion. What comes to mind when you hear that word? Dedicated athletes? Mothers protecting their young? Revivalists? Helping the poor? Lovers of fine art? Mission trips? Sex?

Passion is a vital part of who we are. We are made in the image of our passionate Father, and He is crazy about each one of us! He wants us to be passionate, and He often uses our passions to propel us into His plans for us and our futures.

As one of the 7 Secrets of enjoying a supernatural marriage, passion is your passport into the land of love—vibrant, alive, rousing love. You can be filled with passion for God and for your mate, hearts overflowing toward both. You can be a red-hot lover! Your heart can beat in sync with the very heartbeat of heaven. Loving God. Loving others. Passionately.

A beautiful example of this powerful passion is seen in a stallion. Dan spent several years training and showing Arabian horses. They are magnificent animals and are highly valued around the world. You are very much like this beautiful, amazing beast. And ladies, since men are included in being the bride of Christ, we give you permission to consider yourself a stallion as you read the following descriptions.

Passion Is a Stallion

His white coat shimmers in the spotlight as all four feet prance in place. With nostrils flaring, the stallion snorts yet again—frustrated that the rider will not allow him to run. He is a powder keg ready to explode into action as the large green gate of the arena swings open.

As horse and rider enter the arena, the stallion snaps to attention. With ears turned forward and eyes glistening, he is fully alert and ready to perform. Each animated step displays energy and precision. This is a powerful animal whose every move is controlled by unperceivable signals from the skilled rider astride. A touch from the reins tucks the stallion's head into the perfect position. A squeeze from both thighs says, "Lift your hooves still higher." The horse is spirited but gentle. His performance is an awesome show to behold.

On the other hand, the phrase "unbridled passion" speaks of one who has the energy and enthusiasm of a show horse but lacks the willingness to respond to any form of control. This animal is dangerous and can even be deadly to others who share the arena. Owners often leave poorly trained stallions locked in their stalls, where they become still harder to work with because there is no outlet for the passion within.

Sometimes we are afraid of the passions within us and try to ignore them by locking them out of our thinking and removing them from our life experience. This results in the same kind of danger as that of a stallion confined to his stall. An explosion of pent-up energy is almost certain to occur. Passion released in this way is never a pretty picture.

Another way to deal with stallions that are out of control is to geld them. Castration will remove passion in a way that it will never return. Unfortunately, the ability to put on a spirited show is also gone forever. A gelded stallion will not win the trophy at the end of the show.

We must not allow our God-given passions to be removed or destroyed. They are essential if we are to receive the prize for which God has called us heavenward (Philippians 3:14).

God places passions within every one of us. You may have been told that what you are passionate about is not useful, practical, or valuable. Others have invalidated your passions and you unwisely accepted their opinions—excluding the opportunity to experience what your heart has always longed for. It is as if the very thing you were desperate for was surgically removed from your life. God wants to restore every passion you were created to satisfy in your life and in your marriage.

The magnificent show stallion did not begin training the day before he pranced into the arena. His training started years before.

The day a colt was born, Dan would go to its place of birthing and put a halter around its head. Without fail, his pulling the colt forward by the rope would result in a vigorous tug-of-war.

With its young age, Dan was easily able to overpower the new-born foal. Soon it would realize that Dan was the stronger one and would follow him wherever he led.

This was the first step in the gentling process. When the colt grew to become a thousand pounds of powerful stallion, it still believed Dan could win the tug-of-war. The horse had learned to obey so well that its passion could be bridled, making it useful to the one in authority. Though it remained a spirited stallion, the horse could accomplish everything it was created to do because it was responsive—beautifully under its rider's control.

No other person has ever carried the degree of passion we see in the life of Jesus. Yet He was as gentle as a lamb. Jesus shows us the beauty of being gentled by the one who trains us. He said, "Take my yoke upon you and learn from me, for I am gentle and humble in heart, and you will find rest for your souls" (Matthew 11:29). The Greek word translated as "gentle" here is *praos* (gentleness of spirit).

God wants you to embrace your passions and allow them to be used for their intended purposes. He will gentle your spirit and guide you along the path to the most magnificent ride you can imagine. Both you and your marriage will be blessed when you allow God to make you gentle, activating every passion He has placed within you.

Risk Worthy

Is it safe to express the passions that we discover within? Every one of them is a gift from God we are meant to use and enjoy.

The passions God has shared with us can and should be for our good. He is the most loving of fathers and gives only good gifts to His children (Matthew 7:11). The gifts we receive help us know the character of the one who gives them.

There is a memorable scene in *The Lion, the Witch and the Wardrobe* that reveals much about Jesus—our powerful and passionate King.

"Aslan is a lion—the Lion, the great Lion."

"Ooh," said Susan. "I'd thought he was a man. Is he quite safe? I shall feel rather nervous about meeting a lion."

"Safe?" said Mr. Beaver. "Who said anything about safe? 'Course he isn't safe. But he's good. He's the King, I tell you."[1]

Our passionate God is very much like Aslan. He may not always feel safe, but He is always completely good. There is a sense of risk we feel when pursuing God with all our heart, mind, and strength. The enemy is afraid of true passion in God's people and wants us to join him in his fear. The perfect love of God in you will destroy that fear completely.

Always playing it safe is the direct path to relational mediocrity. You do not want a mediocre love relationship with God, nor do you want this with your mate. God designed men and women to passionately come together in marriage, experiencing intimacy beyond that of any other human relationship. Yes, there is risk in loving one another. Embracing the passions God has placed within you will always involve risk. But there is no safer place to be.

---

1 C. S. Lewis, *The Lion, the Witch and the Wardrobe* (New York, NY: HarperCollins Publishers, 1978), 79–80.

Risking Being Vulnerable

Be naked and unashamed (Genesis 2:25) with both God and your partner in marriage.

This phrase is as much about exposing your inner self as it is about revealing your uncovered skin. This phrase reminds you to share the deepest of your inner thoughts with the one you love. Allow your mate to know you as you really are. Remove the masks. Break down the facades. Simply be yourself. It is exhausting to pretend to be someone other than who you truly are.

Risking Sharing Your Emotions

Be sure to let your partner know when you are joyful, pleased, and content. And yes, be honest by sharing that you feel anxious, lonely, or sad. Jesus was free in expressing His emotions. He wept in front of others when Lazarus died (John 11:35) and was justifiably angry with the money changers in the temple (Matthew 21:12).

Emotions in themselves are neither good nor bad. You can trust God to lead you in the best way to express them. You must not be ruled by your emotions. But sharing them well within marriage will add intimacy and bring understanding. Emotions become life giving when shared wisely with the one you love.

Risking Being Free with Your Body

You are fearfully and wonderfully made (Psalm 139:14), a delight to your lifelong lover. Your body was created to bring both you and your partner great pleasure in lovemaking. Freely enjoy one another using every one of your senses.

We believe the only source of true passion is God. Because He is good, passion cannot be evil. Passions are useful for good when your life is within His control. But unbridled passions can bring great damage to both you and your mate.

Satan is out to steal, kill, and destroy your life, and your marriage as well (John 10:10). He is expert at twisting something intended for good into something that is used for evil. Examples of misapplied passion abound in the world in which we live.

Be sure that God is the one driving your passions and teaching you how to use them.

Discernment is of great value in a marriage that is supernatural. Listen to your partner. Trust his or her advice. Heed the wise council of your godly companion.

Your passions will not be the same as those of your mate. It will take patience and kindness to meld them together. Do not place your personal desires in a higher position than those of your partner. Always do what is best for your marriage.

Most of all, love each other as if your life depended on it. Love makes up for practically anything (1 Peter 4:8). You must be passionate about love.

Love, Love, Love, Love

What is love in the truest sense of the word? Romance novels often portray "love" relationships that are not true love at all. When our passions are linked with things that are not good for us—selfishness, manipulation, control—they become a very destructive force in our lives. But when passion is bridled by the pure love of God, it can propel us into relational intimacy beyond what we have imagined. Taking the risk of loving with passion can be the critical step that leads to experiencing the ultimate satisfactions in life. Passion can be completely safe when solidly bound to love.

Love is the central passion of relational intimacy. We all have access to the supernatural love that flows into us straight from the heart of God. To understand this better, let's explore the words from New Testament Scripture that are translated in our Bibles as "love."

When asked by someone what the "greatest commandment in the Law" was, Jesus responded by saying, "'Love the LORD your God with all your heart and with all your soul and with all your mind.' This is the first and greatest commandment. And the second is like it: 'Love your neighbor as yourself.' All the Law and the Prophets hang on these two commandments" (Matthew 22:34–40).

As we learn to love God, He imparts to us the ability to love our neighbors as we love ourselves. And who could possibly be a closer neighbor than your spouse? We greatly honor God when we honestly and consistently love our mates.

From the beginning it has been God's desire that we "should love one another" (1 John 3:11). His will is no different now than it was in the garden of Eden. Our ability to love, both in and beyond our marital relationships, is the primary indicator of the validity of our connectedness with God. The apostle John states this quite clearly:

Dear friends, since God so loved us, we also ought to love one another. No one has ever seen God; but if we love one another, God lives in us and his love is made complete in us. … God is love. Whoever lives in love lives in God, and God in him. (1 John 4:11–12, 16)

When we are saved, the Holy Spirit enters us and lives inside of us. God Himself, who is love, actually exists within our spirits, and love itself becomes a prominent part of who we are. The supernatural presence of God in us changes the desires of our hearts, altering the way we think, speak, and behave. Most importantly, the entrance of God into our very being enables us to live and dwell "in love."

The New Testament writers used the Greek word *agape* to help explain the perfect love of God intended to flow through each person involved in marriage. This is the type of love described so beautifully and poetically in 1 Corinthians 13. In fact, by inspiring this glorious chapter defining *agape* love, God perfectly describes Himself. *Agape* love is the essence of who God is. It is the solid rock upon which holy matrimony is built. Paul writes:

Love is patient, love is kind. It does not envy, it does not boast, it is not proud. It is not rude, it is not self-seeking, it is not easily angered, it keeps no record of wrongs. Love does not delight in evil but rejoices with the truth. It always protects, always trusts, always hopes, always perseveres. Love never fails. (1 Corinthians 13:4–8)

Agape is selfless and giving. Its motives are completely pure. *Agape* looks to the needs and desires of others in relationship with us and it demonstrates patience and kindness while wrapping its possessor in a cloak of humility. One who is filled with *agape* forgives easily, enabling the release of injuries from the past with a fully open hand. A spouse filled with the *agape* of God maintains hope even in situations where logic would dictate despair, knowing we will not be disappointed by hope. "And hope does not disappoint us, because God has poured out his love into our hearts by the Holy Spirit, whom he has given us" (Romans 5:5).

The secular world celebrates *eros,* which is romantic and sensual love, as being of primary importance in establishing and maintaining a marital relationship. *Eros,* by itself, is an unreliable foundation upon which many marriages and families are built. It can be passionate and strong, but its intensity varies significantly over time. *Agape* is stable, reliable, and eternally valuable in all human relationships. It produces a marriage that is not threatened by the circumstances of life or the winds of time. When received as a gift from God, *agape* can be as unchanging as the Giver Himself.

A third word for love from Greek linguistics is *phileo.* This form implies the affectionate love shared between the closest of friends, written about in Proverbs 18:24: "A man of many companions may come to ruin, but there is a friend who sticks closer than a brother." It is used to express shared fondness between two people who truly enjoy being together. *Phileo* can and should be strongly evident in the marital relationship. Ever since we met in the medical school library, Linda and I have each considered the other to be our dearest friend.

The fourth type of love is *storgos,* which is a love that exists between family members. God has placed within each of us a particularly strong desire to remain connected to our earthly family. These relationships are so notable they were included in the short list of the Ten Commandments etched in stone on Mount Sinai: "Honor your father and your mother, so that you may live long in the land the Lord your God is giving you" (Exodus 20:12). Even secular society honors a particularly strong bond between family members, as is demonstrated by the expression "Blood is thicker than water."

Agape, eros, phileo, and *storgos* are all clearly evident in supernatural marriage. The consistent presence of all four kinds of love secures the couple's bond by providing joy, satisfaction, and stability. Each spouse feels completely loved and totally accepted by the other. This is God's desire for all His married children.

Emulate All Dimensions of Love

We know a couple who exhibits all four dimensions of love. They passionately love each other and God. John and Deborah (names changed to protect them) are dear friends in China. John is a successful businessman and a great husband and father. This supernatural couple has a cute little daughter, and she is their only child due to the nation's one-child-per-couple policy. They also take care of John's aging mother.

In the midst of their busy lives they oversee an organization of underground house churches. We have had the privilege of meeting with them a few times. It is hard to imagine any worship being more passionate than theirs. The Chinese may not be as loud or exuberant as some other cultures, but their praise and prayers are amazing!

Every time we have seen John and Deborah, we have been moved by their deep love and tenderness toward each other, and their devotion to the Lord. They inspire us!

Surely Not

Years ago we were part of a three-couple panel discussing marriage and fielding questions from the audience in a big church. One of the other couples on the panel had been married fifty years. After the discussion, we were backstage chatting with them. The woman turned to us and said with venom in her voice, "If I had to do it over again, I wouldn't!" We were shocked!

Their love was weak, their passion gone. How tragic that this couple had endured each other for half a century only by being committed to the commitment. They were stuck. Did this union bring glory to God? Sadly, it did not. Yet even at this point in their lives they could still change!

Supernatural marriage does not have to begin in the honeymoon phase of life. God can and does instantly, suddenly, surprisingly transform passionless marriages. He is a miracle-working God today, and He desires even more than you that your marriage be full of richness and beauty.

Synonyms and Antonyms for Passion

We find the synonyms and antonyms of passion very interesting. Consider them with us.

Synonyms (words with similar meaning) of passion include *intense, rousing, stirring, blazing, deep, inspired, powerful, profound, zealous.*

As you might expect, antonyms are words with opposite meanings. We can learn much about passion by looking at its opposites: *apathetic, calm, cold, cool, dispassionate, dull, indifferent, unconcerned.*

Do you see these synonyms and antonyms for passion in the two stories we just told? Which set of words paints a picture of your marriage? And which describes your relationship with the King of the universe? Unlike the elderly couple above, you can choose to live your life with passion. It is a choice, you know. Regardless of your spouse, you can choose passion— deeply and freely loving both your mate and your God.

Cravings

We are passionate about the things we crave. As a wife or husband, what do you crave the most in marriage? Is it sex? A good back scratch? Foot massages can be nice. Perhaps you long for time together, vulnerable conversations, long walks as the sun sets, or an action-packed adventure together.

There is great variety in the things we crave. Every one of them adds a little zest, a touch of spice to our lives. Honestly share what you are passionate about with your partner, and be willing to act on his or her yearnings that are different from your own. It's a way of saying, "I love you," without speaking a single word. This will bless your union and bring joy to both of your hearts. Marriage is made stronger as each healthy desire is fulfilled.

> Sustain me with cakes of raisins,
> Refresh me with apples,
> For I am lovesick. (Song of Solomon 2:5 NKJV)

Every husband and wife has a passionate need for love. Note that this is a *need,* not just a *desire.* We long to be loved by another. We yearn to express love and have it fully received. God created marriage to be a place where we can live in contentment, the passions within us carrying out His good plan.

> All night long on my bed
>   I looked for the one my heart loves;
>   I looked for him but did not find him. …
> Scarcely had I passed them
>   when I found the one my heart loves.
>   I held him and would not let him go.
> (Song of Solomon 3:1, 4)

Note that in this passage it is the woman who is doing the chasing and the catching. It is also she who commits to holding on.

Both men and women crave to pursue and be pursued with

passion. And both truly want to be caught. Passionately pursue your mate in a way that he or she can receive your advances and not be repulsed by them. Hold on for dear life. Never let go of the love God has given the two of you to share.

The beautiful poetry we read in Song of Solomon is much more than a romantic story of a woman and a man. It is an allegory about us as the bride of Christ and Jesus as the ultimate Bridegroom. Our primary passion must be focused on God (Father, Jesus, and Holy Spirit—the Triune God who is one) above all other lovers. He has a godly jealousy for us (2 Corinthians 11:2) and demands that we love Him first. Yet He is pleased when we also love one another.

God has placed His passions in you—and in your partner as well. He gave these gifts to each of you so that your lives would be filled with abundance. Drink deeply from the Living Water. Invite your Father to fill you with His perfect love. "Delight yourself in the LORD and He will give you the desires of your heart" (Psalm 37:4). It is *His* passion that all of *your* passions be satisfied.

Again and Again

Who better demonstrates passion than a child? Our granddaughter exhibited passion for play once when we were visiting. We were sitting on the sofa as she ran a circle around the living room, then jumped onto the sofa for Papa D to tickle her. After a moment of tickling she hopped off the couch and said, "Again?" This went on—again and again and again—so long that she could no longer climb up onto the sofa for the tickle.

Our Father loves it when we delight in Him! He loves to say yes to all our agains. "Abba, can we tell You again how much we love You? Daddy, may we daydream with You one more time? Father, will You show us more of Your glory? Again, Daddy, again!"

The same holds true with our mates. "Can I tell you again, honey, that I love you? May we dream and scheme together once again, dear? Hey, Babe, can you hold me just one more time?" Passion says yes to the agains.

You don't have to know the whats, hows, and whys. Go after a supernatural marriage with passion. More importantly, go after God. He will supply the passion. He will lovingly and effectively provide everything you need as you run to Him. He will lift you in His strong arms, and He might even tickle you a little as you go to Him again and again. He is passionate about you!

7 Secrets Suggestion

In a private place, light a candle, turn off the lights, and cuddle as you pray together with your spouse. Experience the warmth of God's gentle caress as you welcome Him into the center of your marriage.

SECRET 3: PRESENCE

God is love. As you and your mate intimately experience Him, the extravagant love of heaven will flow into and through your marriage.

Are you ready for the ride of your life? Are you ready for understanding your depth of purpose and calling? Are you ready for the knowing in your heart and in your mind that God really is good, all-powerful, and full of love? Are you ready to *feel* His intimate love for you? Well, friend, the secret to bringing these blessings into your life and marriage is found in the supernatural presence of the living God. As you and your mate linger in His presence, the extravagant love of heaven will flow into and through your marriage, filling your hearts and your home with love, peace, and joy.

Do the promises mentioned above sound too good to be true? Stay with us here. Once you have made Jesus your Lord, you will want to follow Him. Passion then propels you into wanting more and more of God in your life. You become crazy in love with this astounding King of all kings. And then your desire becomes desperate for Him, for His presence. You simply want to be with Him all the time. Moses and other fathers in the Bible learned this secret. Moses even told God that he didn't want to go anywhere without His presence (Exodus 33:15).

Picture young, happy children. This sweet little boy and precious little girl love, love, love to sit in Daddy's lap. Dad comes home from work to enjoy a nice rest in his big chair after supper. Before he knows it, his lap is full of children snuggling up to his chest. Ahhhh. This is a highlight of his day!

Sometimes they ask questions, sometimes they tell him about all the exciting events of their day, and sometimes they are content to sit quietly—so quietly that they can even hear his heartbeat. While sitting in Daddy's lap, all is right with the world. The children know without question that they are safe and loved. They know that Daddy is big and strong; he will protect them and provide for all their needs. Their hearts are full. And so is his.

When we first began to experience the tangible presence of God's Spirit, we received revelation of the reality and depth of His astonishing love. Our Daddy, Abba, really did want to be with us! And we passionately wanted to be with Him. Understanding that our Father, the one and only mighty, omnipotent God, actually enjoyed being with us rocked our world.

God's presence, this secret to supernatural marriage, will change your heart and your home. We promise.

The richest and most intimate revelations from God must first be experienced in the flesh before they can be even partially understood by the mind. Our flesh is useful in demonstrating the glory of the Lord, but it can in no way contain it. When the Holy Spirit fills us, our bodies can and often do respond in extraordinary and unexpected ways. These responses do not always accompany the presence of God, but quite frequently they do.

Bodily responses such as tears, laughter, shaking, and losing the ability to stand are manifestations in the natural realm of supernatural events. These unexpected ecstatic experiences are simply outward signs of the Lord doing deep, significant things inside: restoring peace, giving direction, revealing purpose and destiny, convincing you of His love for you. My friend, this is good!

Fear of losing control, fear that someone might observe our bodies being out of control, and simple unbelief were the primary reasons we resisted the Holy Spirit and His touch for decades. In the next chapter, we will tell you how God set us free from these hindrances, but for now we ask that you trust us that the benefits of giving Him free reign in all areas of life are totally worth it. He, remember, is not safe, but He is very good.

Why Presence?

By this point you might be wondering, "Why do my partner and I need to pursue God's presence? Isn't the Holy Spirit in us already?

God is omnipresent. He is present in all places at the same time, all the time. Even unbelievers are always in the presence of God—to a degree. Yet there is more to this presence than yes or no. There are different levels of intensity and different ways in which God chooses to present Himself to us as His children.

Over 3,000 years ago Moses first experienced the manifest presence of God in the burning bush in the desert near Mount Sinai (Exodus 3:4). Then, as Moses and the Israelites fled Egypt, His presence was with them in a new and special way—the pillar of cloud by day and the pillar of fire each night (Exodus 13:21). All Israel was aware of this dramatic manifestation of God's presence.

Later on God demonstrated His presence with intensity to Moses and the people by appearing in the clouds as a consuming fire on Mount Sinai (Exodus 24:17). During his most intimate encounter with the presence of God, Moses actually saw the glory of the Lord pass by (Exodus 33:22). Every time Moses entered the perceivable presence of God, he left a changed man. Through each experience Moses was further prepared to play his part in God's glorious plan.

Even Jesus, who certainly walked in the presence of the Father every day of His earthly life, stepped into a higher level of walking in that presence during His baptism in the Jordan River. The Spirit of God descended like a dove and lighted on Him (Matthew 3:16)—reminiscent of the ancient prophecy "The Spirit of the LORD will rest upon him" (Isaiah 11:2). Jesus was immediately "filled with the Spirit" in a new and remarkable way (Luke 4:1).

The intense presence of God, visibly seen in the form of a dove, was much more than something Jesus experienced. The

Spirit of God entered Him in a powerful way that changed his capacity to be led by the Father through the years to come. Jesus had already been on earth in the Father's presence for thirty years. Yet in receiving this particular gift of the Spirit, Jesus was transitioned into an even higher plane of living. The Holy Spirit resided inside of Him with a level of intensity never before seen in man. This is a divine mystery.

Jesus was then fully prepared to spend forty days alone, fasting and praying in the wilderness, to triumph over every one of satan's strong temptations, and then to immediately begin three years of the most astonishing ministry ever seen by man.

Yes, Christians all experience the presence of God. He promises that all who are saved will receive the gift of the Holy Spirit. But there are different levels of intensity in the ways God chooses to reveal His glorious presence to us. Every level of His presence has a purpose. Every kind of experience we have with Him changes who we are. Every time we are touched by His glorious presence, we are being prepared and empowered for life events that are about to unfold.

An Early Encounter

While our sons were still living at home, we were immensely blessed to travel to Israel with them and our dear friends and their three sons. Our oldest has been on many trips, but he still says that Israel was his favorite, next to his honeymoon. Being in the Holy Land is life altering.

One of the places we visited in Jerusalem was the Praetorium floor. You can read about this place in Matthew 27. Immediately after Jesus' trial with Pilate, He was led to the Praetorium, where the soldiers stripped him, mocked him, and placed the crown of thorns on His head. From there He was taken to the cross. Many Bible scholars believe that this particular floor in Jerusalem was that place.

As you can imagine, many Christians from all over the world want to go there. When we went, we noticed it was quieter than many of the other holy sites in Israel. There was a sense of sobriety among the crowd. The silence was broken as a tour group from Germany began to sing. We do not understand German, but we recognized the song because it was an old hymn: "Oh sacred head now wounded, with grief and shame weighed down, now scornfully surrounded, with thorns Thine only crown."[2]

Tears came as His sweet presence filled the room. Dan and I clung to each other as we cried, slowly melting down to the ground together on the floor where precious Jesus suffered for us. It was a holy moment. The Holy Spirit communed with us as we praised Him. Jesus' name Emmanuel means "God is with us." And in that moment, He was. Angels gathered in awe. Nothing, nothing is more precious than His presence.

Experiencing Presence

God sometimes touches us in the subtlest of ways. It is similar to what a woman experiences after eighteen to twenty weeks of

2 Words by Bernard of Clairvaux, 1153; translated from Latin to German by Paul Gerhardt, 1656.

pregnancy when she first becomes aware of her baby's movement. A wispy sensation that feels like a feather stroke is suddenly recognized as a kick from little toes. Each successive kick becomes easier to recognize.

The touch from God is much like this.

At church a few years ago, Dan noticed a shivering sensation in his neck and arms. Curiously, the room was not cold. As he worshipped, the shivers increased. Realizing that this was a tangible touch from the Lord, Dan began saying thank you to Him. With each acknowledgement the intensity of the "shiver" grew.

The Holy Spirit likes being recognized and appreciated.

Recently, Linda was walking alone in Kotzebue, Alaska, on the frozen Bering Sea—white as far as the eye could see. Beyond the sea, snow-covered mountains were in view. They rose majestically with the clear, blue sky behind them.

The beauty was stark. The frozen sea was covered in miniature ice sculptures all made by the finger of God. The snow and ice sparkled brilliantly in the sunshine as if it were a blanket of diamonds. And it was quiet. Wondrously quiet.

Alone on the ice, she was overcome by the splendor of the scene. It spoke volumes about the greatness of God. In the middle of nowhere, He was there. Omnipresent. Magnificent. Standing solitary on the ice, she was enveloped by Him. As soon as Dan was free, we hurried back to the frozen ocean. Together on the ice, we were awestruck by the majesty of God. It was a holy moment.

God's presence was weighty on us as we walked along the ice. We could sense that He was enjoying us as much as we Him.

Communion was occurring—His Spirit with ours. A deposit from heaven was implanted deep within our souls.

Practicing the Presence

We have a tradition to pray together every night just before we go to sleep. Praying together used to be awkward and uncomfortable for us, but after entering supernatural marriage, it has become a favorite event that we look forward to every night.

One day Linda had spent time intently focused on enjoying the presence of God. That night in bed, she placed her hand on my (Dan's) chest, asking that anything she had received from the Spirit that day be given to me. As she prayed, my body reacted with strong abdominal contractions and movements I chose not to control. I could feel the holy presence of God deep within my flesh.

For several minutes I lay motionless on the bed, basking in the precious peace only found in God's manifest presence. Then the Spirit rose up within me and I touched Linda with my hand, inviting the Holy Spirit to fill her with more and more of His glory. We prayed like this with each other for some time that night, until our bodies were nearly exhausted. Though we prayed together deep into the night, we awoke the next morning completely refreshed.

During the following weeks we were compelled almost nightly to share the presence and perception of God's Holy Spirit. It would come at some times as a gentle touch; at other times it would arrive as a series of intense waves. On a few occasions these ecstatic bodily sensations would suddenly come upon us both without a word being spoken.

The times in which we experienced these intense perceptions of God's presence were generally followed by long periods of indescribable peace. Sometimes we explain these inexplicable responses to the Holy Spirit as "speaking in tongues with our bodies." Using these periods of enhanced awareness of His tangible presence, God has etched in our minds the concept written of in Psalm 84 by the Sons of Korah. "My soul yearns, even faints, for the courts of the LORD; my heart and my flesh cry out for the living God" (Psalm 84:2). As our flesh has cried out for the living God, He has repeatedly answered with awesome displays of His love, power, and profound peace.

There have been other times when the weighty presence of God has come on both of us at the same time while worshipping together in a church or conference setting. When this occurs, it is certainly possible to resist the relaxed feeling in our bodies and continue to stand. We have found, however, that the intensity of our experiencing God's manifest presence increases if these sensations are welcomed and not refused. Again, God could choose to overpower us without our permission, like He did to Paul on the road to Damascus, but the Holy Spirit loves to be welcomed and honored in our lives.

As the perception of God's supernatural touch grows, it becomes progressively more difficult to remain standing. Sitting down is a common first response, but it often reaches the point at which it is difficult to remain in any position other than lying down across chairs or on the floor. Although this can happen quickly at times, resulting in a literal fall, it often occurs with us slowly and progressively. Ruth Ward Heflin referred to this response to God's presence as "falling into greatness."

At times we both wind up in graceless horizontal positions as we yield our bodies to the presence and power of God's Spirit. We refer to this surprising and powerful interaction with the Holy Spirit as "melting." Just like a good chocolate bar left in the car on a hot, sunny day, our bodies slowly melt in response to the presence of the Holy Spirit.

This happened quite forcefully to us once during the evening worship time at a Christian conference. We stopped singing for a moment because we felt led to pray for each other. In a totally unplanned and unexpected way, we both melted down into our chairs, ending the service awkwardly as we slumped against each other. Due to the overwhelming presence of God, we were hardly aware of our surroundings. We remained in that odd but pleasant state for an extended period of time. When we were finally willing and able to get up to leave, only a handful of people remained from the hundreds who had previously been there. This was a major encounter for both of us with the tangible presence of God's Holy Spirit. It was one of the most powerful and memorable supernatural experiences of our lives!

We have learned that giving and receiving the presence and gifts of the Holy Spirit is meant to be a regular part of our everyday lives. Significant encounters with God can and do occur in casual settings. The sharing together of spiritual experiences with a marital partner is a practical and nonthreatening way to learn how to participate in the supernatural realm. The intimate ambiance of marriage is the ideal setting for a man and woman to feel the intimacy of God's loving touch.

The frequency of these one-flesh interactions with God as a couple is not always on a daily basis, yet it is not unusual for them to be part of our shared worship and prayer. We can choose to enter His presence in this tangible way almost at will. We can intentionally step into the divine glory of His manifest presence. His touch will be made available to those who keep asking, who keep seeking, and who keep knocking (Matthew 7:7). The intensity and satisfaction of intimacy with God is surprising and amazing, actually surpassing what can be enjoyed from physical intimacy in marriage.

Presence in the Night

Boy, oh boy, is it ever fun when the Holy Spirit surprises us with something new! May we share a couple of Linda's stories with you?

Recently we were on a long flight home from New Zealand to Fort Worth. Dan's lower back had been bothering him for several months. Frankly, we were concerned that sitting many hours across the Pacific could bring him much pain.

After getting all settled into our seats, we put on our eye masks, hoping for some sleep. While sleeping I had a dream in which a blue cloud of electricity massaged Dan's back. It was beautiful as it moved up and down, left and right, touching every sore muscle and nerve. Then, poof, it was gone.

I awakened before Dan and was remembering the dream when he awoke. Without me saying anything first, he turned to me and said, "Wow! My back feels great. I feel better than I have felt in months." Yippee! A moment of Holy Spirit massage did more than months of exercising. What a blessing! And how sweet of God to show me what He was doing in my dream. We love to live in His presence.

Another time, God awakened me in the middle of the night. Dan was sleeping when a brilliant white light suddenly appeared in our bedroom. I saw a dazzling white cloud hovering over him. It was inches above his body, reaching from head to toe, and almost touching our ceiling. This cloud was so bright that I had to turn my face from it. Surprisingly, after this encounter I simply went back to sleep.

The next morning I excitedly asked Dan if he had felt anything in the night or had any dreams. No. Nothing. Nada. *What's up with this, Lord?*

Later we were talking with James Goll, telling him about this glory cloud. He said that God was imparting something to Dan that he needed, and that I was blessed with the gift of seeing it due to my prayers for Dan. Supernatural marriage! We both get to share the beauty of what God is doing in us, and we each get to celebrate when one or the other receives a touch from the Lord.

Pursuing Presence

We were all created to pursue the presence of God and to be blessed through every encounter. In what setting are you most apt to recognize God's supernatural presence? Do you regularly place yourself in this situation? Below are suggestions of some things you can do that will be helpful in your pursuit:

Join with others. Be regularly involved in the worship and ministry of the local church you have joined. Small groups within your church and other gatherings of believers are a wonderful opportunity to connect with others who are also seeking the presence of God. Find friends who are passionate about Jesus. As iron sharpens iron, so you can sharpen one another (Proverbs 27:17).

Get alone with God. Better yet, make it a threesome by inviting your mate! Go on a date and spend some quality time together. Remember the promise spoken by Jesus: "When two or three of you are together because of me, you can be sure that I'll be there" (Matthew 18:20 *The Message*).

Observe nature. A walk in the gentle rain, dazzling colors at sunset, waves in the moonlight, a falling star just for fun—all can be seen in the astonishing natural creation. They are waiting for you to observe, study, and enjoy along with your partner. For in creation, God's invisible qualities—His eternal power and divine nature—can be clearly seen (Romans 1:20). God loves for you to experience Him through nature.

Listen in silence. "Be still, and know that I am God" (Psalm 46:10). The whispers of His loving words can best be heard through silence. Listen. Learn. Love Him in return.

Express awe. Silence is golden as you learn to experience God. But there is also a time to speak words out loud

(Ecclesiastes 3:7). He loves to hear your voice proclaiming praise and thanksgiving, wonder and awe. God is attracted to sincere adoration. When He hears it, He comes.

Invite and welcome. Jesus said, "Which of you fathers [mothers too], if your son asks for a fish, will give him a snake instead? Or if he asks for an egg, will give him a scorpion? If you then, though you are evil, know how to give good gifts to your children, how much more will your Father in heaven give the Holy Spirit to those who ask him" (Luke 11:11–13)! Our Father wants to be invited into your life. When asked, He will share His supernatural presence with you. It is the perfect gift for all occasions.

Soak. Enjoying God's presence is not about effort, it's about receiving Him. Take the time and allow the space for God to reveal Himself to you. A beautiful way to welcome Him is soaking—quietly resting as soft worship music plays in the background. Sometimes the best way to receive is to passively absorb.

We value soaking so highly that we arranged for the album *CHOSEN: You Are My Desire* to be recorded during a Supernatural Marriage event in Dallas, Texas. Four of our favorite worship leaders are featured in this live recording, but there are many others that we enjoy as well. Ask your friends which artists they would recommend. Choose music that touches your spirit and makes you feel intimate with the Lover of your soul.

Pray. One of our favorite ways to be together is cuddling up in bed just before sleep. This can be a very tranquil time, a sweet bedtime routine. But there are times when God chooses otherwise. We have experienced powerful encounters in His presence. Be available to Him for both.

Honor dreams. God has always spoken to His children through dreams. He speaks to your spirit even when your body is fast asleep. We ask God to sanctify our dreams so that they will be lucid and powerful—directly from Him. Share what you see with your partner and interpret your dreams together. God loves to commune with those who honor His dreams.

Attend events. There is no better way for you and your mate to enter God's presence than by joining with others who are pursuing it with passion. Corporate anointing is real. When those who are hungry for the presence gather together, He always comes! Look at the advertising of Christian events. Do they mention God's presence or encountering Him? Ask friends to share what conferences have helped them grow in intimacy.

Intimate Presence

God created marriage to be holy. Husbands and wives are called to relate spirit to Spirit with Holy God. The only path to this kind of intimacy is through the presence of His Spirit. If supernatural marriage is your destination, then the Holy Spirit is the fuel in your tank. You can't get there without His presence.

Seven hundred years before Jesus was born, it was prophesied, "The Spirit of the LORD will rest upon him" (Isaiah 11:2). Following Jesus' ascension, on the Day of Pentecost, the believers who were waiting on the presence of the Lord were filled with the Spirit. It is our desire that the Holy Spirit would both rest upon and fill your life—and your marriage as well.

God desires to be more intimate with you than you are with your marriage partner in lovemaking. He wants to know you, and you to know Him in the richest sense of the word. Because God loves you, He wants His presence to be upon you and in you—His unfathomable love flowing through you.

God joined the two of you to be one in the covenant of marriage. As you become more intimately connected with God, you are also enabled to more intimately relate to your mate. This applies to both the physical, natural relationship and the spiritual, supernatural relationship within marriage. Both you and your partner can become more completely "one flesh" (Genesis 2:24) through the presence of the Holy Spirit.

Psalm 16:11 says, "You have made known to me the path of life; you will fill me with joy in your presence with eternal pleasures at your right hand." This Scripture reminds us of the third secret and the promise available as you walk down the path of life. The promise is for joy and eternal pleasure. We find these in the presence of our God. May you and your mate enjoy both forever.

7 Secrets Suggestion

Try soaking together. Recline in a quiet place. Hold hands. Close your eyes. Listen to worship music. Invite the presence of God and ask the Holy Spirit to allow you to feel His presence together as one.

SECRET 4: POWER

You are not a wimp. You have Holy Spirit power to break free from your past, from bondage to sin, and from ho-hum marriage. God's power enables us to go for the gusto in loving and being loved.

As a child, did you ever play "King on the Mountain"? Linda grew up on a farm and had a big butane tank outside that fueled her mom's stove. Often when playing with her siblings or cousins, they would climb up onto the butane tank, lightheartedly scuffling to see who could remain the last one on top, the king of the mountain.

Jesus is *the* King on the mountain! No one and no thing can topple Him from His rightful position on top. He is the superhero of all heroes. Our God is not a wimp! And His power enables us to go for the gusto in loving and being loved. Life with God is awesome and exciting!

You have progressed from bowing to Jesus as Lord, to pursuing Him with great passion, to resting in His presence. Hallelujah! Each of these steps is needed if you are to receive the next of the *7 Secrets of a Supernatural Marriage—power*!

After Jesus came up from the waters of baptism, the Spirit of God rested upon Him in the form of a dove. He was then filled with the Holy Spirit who led Jesus through a time in the wilderness and His temptation by satan. After overcoming satan, Jesus "returned to Galilee in the *power* of the Spirit" (Luke 4:14, emphasis added) to begin His power-filled years of ministry.

In His life on earth Jesus not only demonstrated the power He had received, He also taught about it. Near Caesarea Phillipi, Jesus told His disciples and the crowd that soon His kingdom would come with power (Greek word *dunamis* in Mark 9:10). In the last moments before Jesus ascended to heaven, He promised His disciples that they would receive *dunamis* power when the Holy Spirit came upon them (Acts 1:8). You and your mate have access to the same Holy Spirit that entered these men and changed their lives forever.

God is able to do immeasurably more than all you ask or imagine (Ephesians 3:20) because His *dunamis* is at work within you. Who does not need or desire more power from God? Nothing will propel your marriage faster or further.

Would you like to see heavenly dynamite blow the limitations off your marriage? Hang on to your hats as we share this amazing secret with you.

Supernatural Power

It is hard to stay in our seats as we write this chapter. We feel the excitement that heaven is experiencing when the sons and daughters of God realize who they are in Christ. The God who did astounding, surprising, unconventional, supernatural acts throughout the Bible is the same today as He was yesterday. Why would we not fully expect Him to perform mighty acts in us and through us today?

In supernatural marriage God delights in showing off His power through the two of you! And if yours is not a supernatural marriage quite yet, be encouraged. His power has not diminished one iota since the days of power encountered in Scripture.

Let your hope and excitement rise as we recall a few of His amazing feats scattered throughout the Bible.

- Genesis 1:27: *God created man in his own image.*
- Genesis 35:5: *The terror of God fell upon the towns all around them so that no one pursued them.*
- Exodus 14:24: *The Lord looked down from the pillar of fire and cloud at the Egyptian army and threw it into confusion.*
- Exodus 17:6: *Strike the rock, and water will come out of it for the people to drink.*
- Joshua 3:13: *As soon as the priests who carry the ark of the Lord—the Lord of all the earth—set foot in the Jordan, its waters flowing downstream will be cut off and stand up in a heap.*
- 1 Samuel 17:45: *David said to the Philistine, "You come against me with sword and spear and javelin, but I come against you in the name of the* Lord *Almighty."*

- 1 Kings 17: 14: *The jar of flour will not be used up and the jug of oil will not run dry until the Lord gives rain on the land.*
- Isaiah 38:8: *I will make the shadow cast by the sun go back the ten steps it has gone down on the stairway of Ahaz.*
- Daniel 3:27: *The fire had not harmed their bodies, nor was a hair of their heads singed; their robes were not scorched, and there was no smell of fire on them.*
- Matthew 8:3: *Immediately he was healed of his leprosy.*
- Mark 10:52: *Immediately he received his sight and followed Jesus along the road.*
- Acts 1:8: *But you will receive power when the Holy Spirit comes on you; and you will be my witnesses in Jerusalem, and in all Judea and Samaria, and to the ends of the earth.*
- 1 John 4:18: *But perfect love drives out fear.*
- Revelation 12:11: *They overcame him by the blood of the Lamb and by the word of their testimony; they did not love their lives so much as to shrink from death.*

The Bible is filled with examples of God's astonishing power. He knows when to be gentle as a lamb. He also knows when to roar like the mighty lion. At His roar the earth trembles and demons flee. And we have all had some demons that needed to pack up and move on out of our lives! Let's embrace the supernatural, raw power of God, breaking free from whatever is entangling us. It is time to be free!

And now Dan will share our story of God's power setting us free.

Supernatural Freedom

Several years ago, Linda went through an afternoon of teaching and prayer focused on deliverance. The Holy Spirit brought to her mind events from childhood that had never really been dealt with or healed. She was enabled to forgive every hurt the Holy Spirit brought to her mind and repent for participating in things that were not of God. Linda was freed from the control of fear of man and also from pride. That night she felt a deep sense of inner peace and an increased level of confidence that she had never sensed before. No doubt about it—something of great significance had occurred within her during the events of the afternoon!

Linda had always been a gentle person who possessed the ability to love people deeply. Following her time in prayer ministry, I could sense that the intensity of the love she shared had entered a new and higher level. She had loved me deeply for years, but suddenly she loved me even more than before. There was a change within her that was hard to explain. Even our sexual intimacy improved dramatically.

I wasn't surprised that Linda had been blessed through her prayer experience, as most people feel a deep sense of joy and peace for a time after intense communion with God. I purposefully watched her week after week to see how long the spiritual high would last. To my amazement, even after months it did not wear off. She was permanently changed by God's power and presence. We both liked it!

I pondered the delightful change that had occurred in Linda and I thought, *Could this help someone like me?* At first she pressured me to try deliverance prayer, but she wisely backed off to allow the Holy Spirit to lead me into the experience. Linda had gone through a profound change in her life. Out of her love for me she wanted me to experience the same. But her words were not what softened my heart. It was the glory of the Lord shining brightly each day from her radiant face that relentlessly drew me into His plan for my life.

In time I ran out of excuses and finally asked our friends to pray with me. The Spirit of Jesus touched me that night in a way I had never been touched before. Unforgiveness was gone and anger faded. I was delivered from much oppression and began to live with more confidence and joy. God blessed me with an upgraded ability to commune in love with Him. I too had been remarkably changed.

Yet Linda and I were still not as free as we desired to be. We have often observed that God heals and delivers us as if we were onions—layer after layer after layer. It was thrilling to see what His power had done in a few short months. But we knew there was much more that was needed. For a spiritual boost we decided to attend a large Christian conference together.

Four days before the event, I was awakened by a short but intense dream that I knew was from God. Years ago I had seen a basketball hoop in the gymnasium of a very legalistic church.

It was blocked by a piece of plywood that was held in place on top of the hoop by a padlocked chain. Sadly, the plywood had been secured in this way to keep neighborhood children from playing basketball in the church gym.

In my dream I saw the plywood and the hoop exactly as I had seen them years before. Suddenly, the chains crumbled and fell to the ground, and the piece of plywood blocking the hoop began to float up into the air. Within seconds it was completely out of view. In a beautiful and dramatic fashion, God was prophetically telling me that the Breaker (Micah 2:13) was coming. This powerful anointing of God's presence for breakthrough would soon lift what had blocked us for years. Winter was passing and springtime would soon come (Song of Solomon 2:11).

Our first days at the conference were a physical, emotional, and particularly spiritual roller coaster. There was a battle raging within us between the forces of light and the powers of darkness—as intense as any we have ever known. Clearly it was time to send the demons packing. During the lunch break, we went, exhausted, to our hotel room for rest. No nap can come close to the refreshment the Holy Spirit brings!

We began praying for each other, telling whatever demons were pestering us that they had to go. And they did! The power of our amazing God wins every time. After our "power lunch" we happily went back to the conference for even more special touches from the Lord. The day had begun as one of the worst we had ever known. It ended by being the best we can remember. It was an unforgettable day, filled with the presence and the power of our astounding God.

In Ruth Ward Heflin's book, *River Glory*, she writes, "God's desire is to take us places we can't ask to be taken because we don't know they even exist. He wants to give us experiences that we could never request because we have never yet even dreamed of them."[3]

We had entered the realm of supernatural marriage without knowing that it even existed. It was beyond anything we had heard of or dreamed. There was no clue of what was to be coming—and soon!

Supernatural Favor

Not long after experiencing this newfound freedom, we traveled to do ministry in China. Surprisingly, we were invited to have dinner with a Communist leader in the capital city, Beijing. Chairman W began the visit by greeting us in a formal meeting room.[4] Sitting at his right and left hand in large, ornate, and very uncomfortable chairs, we sipped tea together while stiffly discussing current events in China.

After thirty minutes of talking through a translator about nothing of real importance, we drove across town to a private government restaurant and health spa. Inside the imposing facility were several dining rooms, each exquisitely decorated with walls covered in gold leaf, beautiful Chinese artwork,

---

3 Ruth Ward Heflin, *River Glory* (Hagerstown, MD: McDougal Publishing, 1999), 56.
4 Due to safety's sake, we must withhold his full name here.

magnificent hardwood tables, and tastefully upholstered chairs. The entire building was immaculate and pristine, artfully designed, and skillfully fabricated.

When we sat down to eat, Linda pulled out a set of bright yellow plastic chopsticks that were attached at one end by the head of a smiling duck. They were meant for small children, but Linda had brought them as a joke to lighten the mood of our time with the Chinese leaders. They laughed, and we laughed along with them, the mood of the meeting completely changing through this one disarmingly silly act. The twelve courses of food presented to us that day were the most amazing we have ever seen. What was more amazing, however, was the change in the direction of our conversation for the remainder of the meal.

For the next two hours, the chairman asked us a series of questions about what it is like to be a Christian in America. He inquired about the definition of terms such as *church, pastor, elder,* and *deacon*. He wanted to know what worship meant and invited us to describe a typical week of church activity. The chairman seemed concerned that allegiance to God might keep Christians from patriotically serving their country.

He asked what we considered to be the most important thing in life. Dan responded, "God is number one." When he inquired what would be next, Dan smiled and said, "Linda is number two." After some laughter, the chairman asked Linda, "What do you think about being number two?" She confidently replied, "I love it! In fact, God is also number one to me. And Dan is very pleased to be number two after God."

The mouth and the eyes of the chairman opened wide. Coming from a society where the Communist government is supreme and men dominate their families, it was shocking for him to hear Linda publicly say, "Dan is number two." Even more surprising to him was the fact that Dan accepted and even encouraged her to consider him in such a position. We went on to explain more about how men and women relate to each other in Christian marriage with mutual respect, resulting in both partners receiving love and honor. We shared with the chairman how this type of marital relationship is beneficial for any society.

This was a delightful and unique opportunity to discuss the treasure of abundant life in God with a powerful Communist leader. It was given to us as a gift, divinely ordained and supernaturally accomplished through weak vessels much like jars of clay. Paul said ordinary people, like us, diffuse the glory of God through their lives and words: "We have this treasure in jars of clay to show that this all-surpassing power is from God and not from us" (2 Corinthians 4:7). Through the power of the Holy Spirit, our relationship with God was maturing. Like Jesus, we were growing "in favor with God and men" (Luke 2:52).

The next morning we left the gilded halls of the wealthy and were led to be with those whose lives were of the opposite extreme. After traveling to the countryside, we spent the day with an underground church, which literally met underground in the shelter of a large cave. In the natural realm they seemed very poor, yet the Spirit of the Lord was upon them;

they enjoyed riches that cannot be measured in either US dollars or Chinese yuan.

During worship in the cave, we noticed a middle-aged married woman whose face shone like that of an angel. She maintained a countenance of peace that belied the challenges of her life. She turned out to be the pastor of that particular underground church. In spite of the hardships she faced, she had everything she needed for life and godliness (2 Peter 1:3). The opportunity we were given to meet and pray with this precious sister was no less significant than witnessing to Chairman W the day before.

The woman's face and life radiated the glory of God for all to see. Neither her poverty nor the oppressive system of government in which she lived could keep the Light of the World from emitting out of every part of her being. It is the intense desire of our hearts to see that same glory shining out of our marriage and from all who pursue the power of almighty God.

Supernatural Healing

The next month, while in Mombasa, Kenya, we saw God's supernatural power displayed in another remarkable way. While snorkeling in the Indian Ocean at low tide, Linda severely injured her left shin when she fell against a coral formation. The wounds bled for hours and left her in a great deal of pain.

By the end of the second day, signs of infection had begun. Several of us surrounded Linda, proclaiming God's desire and miraculous ability to heal diseases of the skin (2 Kings 5:14; Matthew 8:3; 10:8). A Kenyan sister named Nellie, who had a gift for healing, laid her hand on the oozing wounds and prayed that God would stop the infection. Although we had no access to antibiotics, the infection subsided overnight. By the next morning Linda's leg looked remarkably better. Supernatural healing had occurred in her body by the power of God!

With the infection gone we were able to enjoy the remainder of our trip. However, during the long flight home we noticed a lump developing beneath the skin, near the bone of Linda's lower leg. We again prayed for healing, but the bulge increased gradually in size and the pain in the area intensified.

The morning after returning home, we had the leg examined by a local orthopedic surgeon. He lanced the lesion, a deep cyst from the periostium of the tibia bone. The cultures showed no sign of infection, but the cyst continued to exude a steady flow of clear yellow fluid. Twice a week we returned to the physician, and with each visit, he advised us that surgery was the only way to be sure the oozing would stop. We are not against surgery. Dan is a surgeon. But we heard in our spirits to just wait.

Along with several strong brothers and sisters in Christ, we continued daily asking God to supernaturally heal this non-healing wound. Yet after more than a month of daily packing, the constant dripping of fluid continued unabated. The three-year-old daughter of a friend looked quizzically at Linda and asked, "Why is your leg crying?"

Early one Sunday morning we were worshipping together in

the church sanctuary, hours before the first service was scheduled to begin. As we prayed yet again for God to miraculously heal her wound, Linda received the revelation that a demonic spirit had entered her leg and was mocking the power, glory, and healing ability of Jehovah Rapha—the Lord our Healer (Exodus 15:26).

While praying in tongues, the Holy Spirit came upon Dan. With greater confidence and authority than he had ever before experienced, Dan laid his hand on Linda's injured leg and commanded the mocking spirit to leave. With strength and boldness that rose up from within, he prayed over Linda with more power and fervency than ever before. She immediately felt a physical release as the demonic spirit left her body. We both knew something remarkable and divine had occurred in that moment.

Minutes later we removed the bandage from Linda's lower leg. When we dressed the wound earlier, it leaked continually. Now the dripping had completely ceased, never to return. Jesus healed Linda's injury that day, miraculously demonstrating His power over the enemy and over sickness. It was an astounding and joyful experience to share together, as one flesh, this awesome encounter with our true and living God.

Fireball in the Night

God uses miraculous signs and wonders to demonstrate His supernatural power and eternal glory in such a way that they can be perceived in the natural realm. More than a few times we have been completely surprised by the Lord. Some unusual power encounters, things we have never heard of, have come to us, catching us off guard. We were later to discover that others have had similar experiences. May we share one of these with you?

Our brother-in-law was dying. We flew to see him, desperate to tell him once again that we loved him, and more importantly, that Jesus loved him and had died for him.

Never before had we seen the spirit of death so visible and so mean as in that hospital room. With all the lights on, the room seemed filled with darkness.

That night as we were sleeping, something startling happened. The only way we can describe it is that a fireball, about the size of a basketball, hurled down from heaven, hitting Linda in the abdomen. This was not a pleasant sensation. It hit hard and then was gone. What in the world was that? Now wide awake and praying intensely, we were confident that this was a powerful deposit being made from heaven into us.

The next day we were alone in the ICU room alongside our loved one. With everything in us we began rebuking the spirit of death and declaring life, life, life! We were astonished to sense the Spirit of power rising up within us (Isaiah 11:2). A short time later we had to leave, saddened that we had not seen any visible change.

Miraculously, our brother-in-law improved enough to go home. His brother then had an opportunity to be with him a week, each day explaining about Jesus and His love. The final night before this brother had to leave, our brother-in-law gave his heart and life to Jesus. Hallelujah! As sick as he was, he wanted to be baptized that very night. He had too many tubes to consider getting him in the tub—praise God for baptism by sprinkling. Glory!

Our dear family member went to be with Jesus in heaven two months later. During those last weeks he told us more than once that everything was crazy with him in the hospital except when we prayed. In those moments he felt complete peace. The fireball from heaven empowered our prayers, giving our brother-in-law time to receive the Lord Jesus and live his last earthly days in peace. What a beautiful God we serve.

Signs and Wonders in India

Power encounters with our astounding God abounded on a recent trip to southern India. Have you noticed that we really love it when the Lord shows up and shows off? Never do we feel more alive than when we are co-laboring with Him, regardless of the location.

Often when we go on missions we are alone or with a small team, but on this trip we had ten powerful Jesus lovers along. Our ministry's key verse is Job 9:10, "He performs wonders that cannot be fathomed, miracles that cannot be counted." The team was blessed to see this Scripture come alive before our eyes.

We were evangelizing in big cities and small villages. Some of the tiny village churches were smaller than our living room at home, crowded with thirty people all sitting on straw mats on the floor. Other times we were in a large rented hall with

1,200 in attendance. Regardless of the size of the gathering, the Holy Spirit always came. Surprisingly to us, about one third of every audience rushed to the altar, receiving Jesus as their Savior. Hallelujah!

One day during one of the larger meetings, the Holy Spirit communicated to us that He was releasing His harvest angels. Upon hearing this we were totally undone, falling on our faces sobbing as we worshipped this compassionate God who longs to save people. When we were able to raise our heads, we were astonished to see hundreds and hundreds of individuals, mostly of Hindu faith, rushing forward for prayer.

The team went into action, praying for every single person who wanted prayer. Right before our eyes God moved in power. Approximately eight hundred souls were saved in this one event. Many of the healings were later documented medically. An older woman, bent over with severe back deformity and pain, was overjoyed when God began straightening her back. Her granddaughter watched with wonder as this precious woman stood taller and taller. It happened incrementally beneath Linda's hand, and she said it felt like a car being jacked up for a tire change. We were all astounded!

A baby had been born missing several ribs. They grew back! A man who had been told he had only days to live was healed from a brain tumor. Jesus! Many more were healed of all kinds of ailments. After we returned to the States we were told that sixteen new churches had formed and many of these dear people were baptized.

Our beautiful, powerful God is the same today as He was in Bible times. "LORD, I have heard of your fame; I stand in awe of your deeds, O LORD. Renew them in our day, in our time make them known" (Habakkuk 3:2).

God Is Your Power

The *dunamis* of God is your position of strength. Supernatural power is the pivotal secret in your quest for supernatural marriage.

The devil attacks both lives and marriages with discord, disease, addiction, lack. But the power of heaven in you is greater than the strength of your foe (1 John 4:4). From your position in His power you can face, fight, and defeat the enemy. Yes, you can crush satan underneath your feet (Romans 16:20).

And there will be no fear in battles to come, for the Lord will go before you, the God of Israel will be your rear guard (Isaiah 52:12). As God allows you to experience the power of His Spirit, your life and your marriage will be forever changed.

7 Secrets Suggestion

Plan to minister together with your spouse this week. Perhaps you can bake cookies together, then head to the nearest nursing home to share them. Doing seemingly simple things in Jesus' name is of great value (Mark 9:41). Ministry doesn't have to be fancy, expensive, or performed in a foreign land to be a sweet offering to Jesus.

SECRET 5:
TRANSFORMATION

The sign of supernatural marriage is peace. This peace freely flows from the Holy Spirit as He produces fruit in you. Walking in this supernatural peace creates an ambiance of honor in your marriage.

When our younger son was small, he had more than a little trouble with lying. He would look us right in the eye and lie to us. He did it often and really well. We found ourselves praying that he would be caught each time he lied. Because he was so good at it, unsuspecting ones like his Sunday school teacher would not know he wasn't telling the truth.

Little spankings, time-outs, withdrawal of privileges or treats—nothing we did seemed to work as we tried to "cure" him of this maddening habit. Even amidst the lying, we knew that our son was really sweet and tenderhearted. We were baffled.

Soon thereafter, when our son was still quite young, he told us he had given his heart to Jesus and wanted to be baptized. We were thrilled! Dan had a serious father-son talk with him and felt that he understood this decision. He baptized our son that very week in church. Immediately, miraculously, the lying stopped. The Holy Spirit had invaded his young heart, producing divine transformation in an instant. We were amazed!

Just as the Holy Spirit transformed our son, He changes each of us, and He transforms our marriages into the supernatural ones we all desire. The fifth secret of a supernatural marriage is transformation.

Extreme Makeover

We marvel at the beauty of the butterfly. Your marriage can be equally magnificent. Like the caterpillar prior to metamorphosis, much change will be required. Every husband and every wife need the miraculous transformation that comes only from God—an extreme makeover of the heavenly kind.

Transformation is a metamorphosis from who you are to who you were created to be. It alters how you think, what you pursue, the way you live, and your capacity to love. This is much more than altered behavior. It is a change at the very core of your being, a shift in character that does not revert over time.

It is good to try to be a good partner for your mate. But desire and effort will only advance your marriage so far. True change will never come from your human effort alone. Assistance from God is required. You don't want behavioral modification; you need supernatural transformation!

Neither one of us is the same person we married years ago. And we are so glad!

At our wedding, both of us needed a *lot* of transformation. Much more still remains to come.

Every marriage needs change, but where is it best to begin?

Jesus would remind you to not focus on the speck of sawdust in your partner's eye. Rather, pay attention to the plank in your own (Matthew 7:3). In years of counseling we have learned that finger pointing accomplishes nothing. A transformed marriage begins with you.

Let us share with you a story that allows us all to see the miracle of transformation in action.

Visible Transformation

Desperate for transformation, Bill and Joan attended a marriage retreat a few years ago. They made no secret of the fact that they had endured many struggles in their marriage. His fiery temper had led him to two previous divorces and this was her second marriage. But throughout all the drama, and all the intense arguing, Bill and Joan really wanted this marriage to survive. In fact, they did not want mere survival. They wanted their marriage to flourish.

Combined with Bill's anger was a stronghold of belief that he was unlovable. Joan could see the diamond hidden inside Bill's tough exterior. She was determined to chip away at all the debris concealing his sweet, loveable self. And Joan was one of those rare, beautiful women who did everything with passion.

At the close of the retreat, each couple was asked to publicly state before God and the others their love for one another and their commitment to the marriage. It was a powerful, moving experience for all. By the time Bill and Joan finished their turn, there was not a dry eye in the room.

With great love in her eyes, Joan silently began to wash Bill's feet. She dried them with her beautiful, flowing hair. He was totally disarmed. Bill sat in his chair sobbing as he realized the depth of this woman's passion for him. He *was* loveable!

We all watched as his anger melted away. Together we saw his defensiveness disappear like a vapor. Transformation occurred right before our eyes. "Love never fails" (1 Corinthians 13:8).

We took the liberty of changing our friends' names for this book, but "Bill and Joan" continue celebrating marriage today and are still passionate about Jesus. God's amazing love transformed two broken people into one supernatural couple.

The changes God made in Bill and Joan's marriage were truly astonishing. They remind us of the advertising for a popular toy when our children were young. The ad for this changeable gadget began with the words, "Transformers: more than meets the eye." Each toy had the appearance of a simple car or truck, but had an amazing surprise inside. What would it become? The secret was revealed through transformation.

The transformer toy could not change its own shape. But with a few things moved here and other parts moved over there—all by another set of hands—its secret identity would be revealed.

Your marriage can be much like that delightful toy. What

is visible in the now may be quite different from the Creator's full plan. But there is a surprise to come, a discovery of what is waiting to be seen. Only God can do the moving and changing; only He can do the transforming. What a joyful revelation it will be!

The Soul

At salvation we are shifted from the kingdom of darkness into the kingdom of light. We once were lost, and now we're found. Our spirits are fully redeemed in an instant.

On the day of salvation, our *souls*, on the other hand, have only begun to change. And a great deal of change is required. Remember the peeling of an onion? In God's transformation of our souls (mind, will, emotions, and imagination), layer after layer must be removed to complete the process (sanctification). God transforms our souls progressively through the years, with wondrous results in our lives and marriages.

The Mind

"The mind of a sinful man is death, but the mind controlled by the Spirit is life and peace; the sinful mind is hostile to God. It does not submit to God's law, nor can it do so" (Romans 8:6–7). The mind controlled by the Holy Spirit is willing and able to submit fully to Jesus' lordship—it is "life and peace."

We are told in Romans 12:2, "Do not conform any longer to the pattern of this world, but be transformed by the renew-ing of your mind." This transformation is supernaturally accomplished in our minds through the touch of God. Our way of thinking can be so completely changed that Paul confidently proclaims, "We have the mind of Christ" (1 Corinthians 2:16).

The Will

As our wills are transformed by the Spirit of God within us, they too become more and more like Jesus, who declared, "I have come down from heaven not to do my will but to do the will of him who sent me" (John 6:38). God changes the desire of our hearts to become just like that of Jesus when, submitting to the Father, He prayed, "Your kingdom come, *your will be done* on earth as it is in heaven" (Matthew 6:10, emphasis added).

As children of God we, like Jesus, should pray, "Not my will, but Yours be done" (Luke 22:42). With yielding to God's will as the default setting of our lives, obedience rarely becomes an issue. He promises that blessings will follow (Deuteronomy 28).

The Emotions

Through transformation of our emotions we are freed and empowered to use them in the ways that best honor God. Instead of being only reactions to the triumphs and disappointments of life, our emotions become tools that God can use to accomplish His purposes through us. The Holy Spirit must lead us in the use of our emotions just as we allow God to lead us in our thoughts, words, and actions.

It is impossible to develop a true love relationship with God without becoming emotionally involved. It is unimaginable that a bride could honestly express her love to her groom on their wedding day with no emotion in her voice. Passionate love cannot be expressed without emotion. As we grow in intimacy with the Father, He and we become emotionally involved with each other. His emotions become ours in each situation we encounter. We delight in circumstances that bring Him joy and we grieve with God in situations that cause Him sorrow.

Transformed emotions are a powerful tool for building a spectacular marriage.

The Imagination

The imagination is the creative component placed within each of us by our astoundingly creative Maker. The destiny of this gift is that we would participate with God in using it for the strengthening of the kingdom and for the completion of His plan. God demonstrates astonishing inventiveness in both the natural and the supernatural realms. We can connect with God's imaginative nature through prophetic acts, creative writing, storytelling, creative evangelism, visions, and music. It is also of great value to wives and husbands in lovemaking!

God speaks to us often through dreams in the night. We ask Him to sanctify our imaginations that the dreams we remember would only be those from heaven. Through dreams we can receive clear understanding of the past and present as well as prophetic revelation of the future. Just as is often seen in the Bible, dreams are an amazing and powerful means of communication between the created and Creator. If we are to fulfill the purposes for which we were created, we must allow God to transform our imaginations that they can be used in completing His plan.

Evidence

If your soul is being transformed day by day, how will you know? It is in the fruit, dear friend. Transformation may not occur as suddenly as Clark Kent changing into Superman, but change it is. The fruit will be noticed among your family, your coworkers, and most of all by your mate. And they will all want what you have!

Supernatural wives and husbands are filled with the fruit of the Spirit. Paul gives us a list of what this consists of: "The fruit of the Spirit is love, joy, peace, patience, kindness, goodness, faithfulness, gentleness and self-control. Against such things there is no law" (Galatians 5:22–23). These characteristics are produced in our lives through transformation by the Spirit of God—evidence of His character developing in us. This list of fruit illustrates how God treats others in intimate relationships. It also establishes the gold standard of how we should deal with each other in our relationships—especially marriage.

God's qualities are planted and cultivated in us by the Holy Spirit when we allow Him to take up residence in our hearts. The characteristics of this fruit are not ways of living that we learn about and strive for, but supernaturally obtained qualities that are transferred to our inner person. Spiritual fruit will never be produced through human effort alone. It cannot be successfully manufactured or copied. It will only be seen when we are transformed at the very core of our being.

As we are transformed we begin to *possess* the fruit of the Spirit. It is ours and becomes a vital part of who we are. This pleases God, because the fruit of the Spirit is His character. Paul told the Ephesians to be "imitators of God . . . as dearly loved children" (Ephesians 5:1). Every good father has the desire for his children to grow up to be a good representation of him, and God is no exception. It is God's pleasure to change us to become more like Him.

When the fruit of the Spirit is possessed by both husband and wife in a supernatural marriage, the Father is doubly honored and doubly pleased. With these qualities evident in their lives, abundant life flows freely through their relationship:

- Their *love* for each other is without measure.
- Their *joy* together is unrestrained.
- They walk in *peace* that passes understanding.
- They are *patient* and *kind* to each other, even when imperfections creep in.
- It is always assumed the other's intentions are *good*, though it may seem otherwise.
- There is absolute *faithfulness,* with no thought, hint, or joke of infidelity.
- *Gentleness* prevails in their dealings with each other.
- *Self-control* is consistently present.

What a wonderful, safe place to live and play! Living in supernatural marriage beautifully displays what Jesus asked the Father for when He prayed, "Your kingdom come, your will be done on earth as it is in heaven" (Matthew 6:10). Does this sound idealistic, far-fetched, or even extreme? Does the concept of a transformed marriage sound impossible for you in your particular situation?

Even people with good intentions may tell you that no married couple should hope to enjoy the glory of heaven while still living on earth. Jesus, however, looks at you and says, "With man this is impossible, but with God *all* things are possible" (Matthew 19:26, emphasis added). Do you believe that Jesus only said this, or do you believe He really meant it? And do you believe He meant it for *you* and for *your* marriage?

We are confident this kind of marriage is possible. It is not possible through your own striving and trying to be a better spouse. No, supernatural marriage will only come as you give your life away—trusting God with all your mind, will, and emotions—giving Him free reign to transform your heart.

Signs of Transformation

While still taking our first steps together in supernatural marriage, we were driving on an icy highway in Wyoming. We were listening to a recording of Bill Johnson speaking about the time Jesus slept in a boat with His disciples while a squall raged about them on the Sea of Galilee (Luke 8:22-25). Although the disciples were frightened, Jesus maintained complete peace in the midst of the storm. His rebuking and calming of the storm demonstrated Jesus' authority—a miracle performed so the disciples could also be at peace. Bill said that we have authority in any storm of life in which we maintain supernatural peace.

Moments after we heard this revelation, our SUV suddenly twisted out of control on black ice. We went off the road and across the median at full highway speed. As the vehicle slipped sideways, it rolled four and a half times before finally coming to rest on its roof.

As the accident unfolded before our eyes and our bodies were violently beaten against the SUV's interior, we experienced an amazing sense of profound peace. Earlier that month we had both felt the tangible touch of God's perfect love that drives out fear (1 John 4:18). We looked death in the face but were not afraid. In the midst of chaos, peace remained.

Although Dan was injured, no treatment was required. Linda had emergency abdominal surgery on Christmas Eve for a tear in her small intestine. Twice during her week in the hospital, Linda was blessed with angelic visitations. As we left the blizzard conditions and returned to our home in Texas, other miracles occurred. Throughout this challenging journey, we maintained constant, supernatural peace that transcended our understanding (Philippians 4:7). God had granted us, as a couple, authority over this storm.

The sign of supernatural marriage is peace. Unshakeable peace. It freely flows from the Holy Spirit as He produces fruit in you. This is a normal part of your supernatural life with God.

When friends enter our home for the first time, they often comment that they feel a calming sense of peace. We once thought this was something unique about the property we own. Now we believe what they are experiencing is the covenant of peace given to us by God as we have honored His desires for us in our covenantal marriage. Isaiah prophesied, "'Though the mountains be shaken and the hills be removed, yet my unfailing love for you will not be shaken nor my *covenant of peace* be removed,' says the LORD, who has compassion on you" (54:10, emphasis added). God goes on to say through Ezekiel, "I will make a *covenant of peace* with them and rid the land of wild beasts so that they may live in the desert and sleep in the forests in safety" (34:25, emphasis added).

Jesus says in Matthew 18:20, "Where two or three come together in my name, there am I with them." Jesus is the "Prince of Peace" (Isaiah 9:6); if He is with the two of us, then "the peace of God, which transcends all understanding" (Philippians 4:7), will be recognized by those who know us. Just as God's sign for Noah was the rainbow and His sign for Abraham was circumcision, we believe profound peace in the life of a married couple is His sign to the world of their God-ordained, covenantal oneness.

Peace is a reliable sign of transformation in marriage partners. It is the barometer of a supernatural marriage relationship. If you sense that the level of peace in your marriage is falling, figure out why. Talk about it. Pray about it. The Holy Spirit will show you the solution, and your peace will return. Chaos has no place in a marriage built upon Jesus, the Prince of Peace.

Honor

Some years ago we had the privilege of ministering with missionaries serving in a Middle Eastern nation. For their safely it is best that we not refer to the specific country. Our dear friends Dr. Paul and Teri Looney had been asked to do a couple of marriage weekends for these people. We were blessed to tag along to help.

Paul developed a brilliant conflict-resolution tool he calls "Take it to the Cross." Toward the end of the weekend retreat, we asked for volunteers to model this wonderful exercise. One brave couple stepped forward to do it.

Taking it to the Cross requires each person involved in the conflict to first differentiate between their thoughts and feelings pertaining to the issue, then share them with their mate. It is amazing how difficult it is to define feelings and thoughts under duress. Each person is also instructed to give a proposal as to how the conflict should be resolved. This is followed up with a commitment to each other that this issue will not divide them. Beautiful!

At this weekend retreat, the woman initiated the process of taking their conflict to the cross. She began by stating, "The issue is not having air-conditioning." Her feelings were intense. She believed that she would be a better wife, mother, and housekeeper if she were not hot and irritable all the time. With a little coaching from Teri, she did a great job separating her thoughts and feelings. After listening to her, Linda and I had the mind-set that her husband was a jerk for not giving in to this desire.

When it was her husband's turn to present his side of the issue, he easily stated his thoughts. But, as is often the case with men, he had difficulty expressing his emotions about the conflict. Finally he was able to say that her discomfort brought him great pain, making him feel impotent and helpless.

Once she knew that he had really heard her, with his heart and with his mind, the wife calmed down and became peaceful. As she calmed, she was able to better appreciate his reasoning. Knowing her husband listened to her and desired to ease her life in the foreign land made all the difference. She felt honored.

Watching this couple transform right before our eyes was astounding.

As the facts came fully to light, we learned that they had no electricity. Air-conditioning isn't possible without power! They agreed to save up money to buy a generator and a window air-conditioning unit to cool their master bedroom. (In our opinion, that was a very wise room to choose!) We also learned a lesson about not jumping to conclusions without hearing both sides of a conflict.

By taking it to Jesus' cross, their conflict was resolved. He transformed this marriage, restoring peace to their hearts and home.

Walking in supernatural peace and the other fruit of the

Spirit creates an ambiance of honor in marriage. Transformation by the Spirit prepares husbands and wives to listen to each other, respond in love, and respect their partner's needs. To be esteemed is better than silver or gold (Proverbs 22:1).

When has your spouse felt honored or dishonored by you? Do you regularly express words of respect to your mate? Paul teaches us to "honor one another above yourselves" (Romans 12:10). This can only be accomplished through transformation, not mere willpower. In marriage we honor our spouses when, through our words and our actions, we esteem them higher than ourselves.

Advancement into a Supernatural Marriage

The presence of God's Holy Spirit is the key to transformation, both in our personal lives and in our marriages. Supernaturally experiencing God changes our vision of the future, our purpose in life, the way we think, and the way we act. It enhances our ability to give and receive love.

God is very pleased and quite able to advance you and your mate into the supernatural marriage you were created to enjoy. He is an expert at transforming people! He who began a good work in you will carry it on to completion (Philippians 1:6).

> We, who with unveiled faces all reflect the Lord's glory, are being transformed into his likeness with ever-increasing glory, which comes from the Lord, who is the Spirit.
> (2 Corinthians 3:18)

7 Secrets Suggestion

Considering 2 Corinthians 3:18, what transformation has occurred in you, in your spouse, and in the two of you together? Spend some time thanking God for the transformation He has brought about.

SECRET 6: HOLINESS

Holiness. Purity. These attributes are essential in a supernatural marriage. Living this lifestyle is fun!

Where did we get the idea that holiness was drudgery and boredom? Holiness, dear friend, is the next secret for a supernatural marriage. Holiness and purity simplify life. These attributes are essential for living in harmony with our mates and with God. We get to relax and play freely in the atmosphere of holiness.

Without holiness we have to work to keep up our image, work to remember what story we have told, work to try to out-wit God (as if anyone could). Holiness allows us to live without constantly looking over our shoulders. Life without holiness is hard. Life lived in purity and holiness affords us freedom.

Holy Is Fun

While Linda swam laps at our local YMCA, she asked God for a clear message. There was only one day left before we were to teach about marriage, and the pressure was on. We knew something was lacking in our planned presentation but couldn't figure out what it was. Fresh revelation from God was needed, and quickly! We both trusted that God would provide exactly what He wanted the people to hear, and we were not disappointed with what He gave us that day.

Through the years we have learned that hours of gliding through the cool water of the pool can be an enjoyable and productive time for bathing in the loving presence of the Father. While swimming laps, there are virtually no distractions from our communion with God. We can pray blessings on missionary friends living on any continent in the world or intercede for other issues dear to our hearts. While pushing across the surface of the water, we find it natural to commune with Jesus, our Savior and Friend. There is no better place than the deep end of a swimming pool to ask for and receive the living water of the Holy Spirit described by Jeremiah, Zechariah, and John. What more reasonable place to listen to the gentle whisper of God (1 Kings 19:11–12; Psalm 46:10) than in this environment of near silence?

That day in the pool, Linda asked God, "What do You want to say to me for tomorrow night?" As she swam, Linda patiently waited, listening for God's response to her request. After three laps, she distinctly heard the words come into her mind and her spirit: "Holy is fun!" A bit confused, she silently asked what that phrase meant. Again she heard clearly in her mind and spirit the same phrase: "Holy is fun!"

God's Playground

The Holy Spirit brought to Linda's mind a sermon she had heard years before. The speaker related a story about a school playground adjacent to a busy city street. There was no fence separating the two; both children and teachers could sense the danger that was present. In this atmosphere, kindergarten students remained very close to their teacher during recess instead of playing in the big open field. Although this assured their safety, it deprived them of the many areas and activities available on the playground. The children were unable to fully enjoy recess because the playground felt treacherous to them.

The school leaders, aware of the risk of having children play so close to the street, had a sturdy fence constructed around the borders of the playground. Soon the children were running, bouncing balls, swinging, and exuberantly playing on every square inch of the property. They were full of joy and laughter because they had a safe place to play. What had seemed scary to them was now fun because of the barrier that separated them from the dangerous traffic on the street.

Marriage is very much like that properly fenced playground. In the written word of the Bible, by direct revelation, and through the personal leading of the Holy Spirit, God establishes wise, strong, protective barriers around His children's marital playground. All activity within these secured boundaries is righteous and good, conforming to God's perfect will. Anything outside of these boundaries is unholy, unrighteous, and outside of His will. Everything outside is the street we're not allowed to play in because of the danger involved.

Holiness, God, and Marriage

God is completely holy, and it is His will that the marriage covenant be completely holy as well. Holiness is the essence of who He is and what He is. He cannot be anything less than holy. Because it is impossible for Him to change (Malachi 3:6), He cannot and will not act outside of His character. And because we are created in His image, His desire is for us to become like Him, as completely as possible, both as individuals and as marriage partners.

As we grow in holiness, we honor God as our Creator and honor the beauty and perfection of His plan. Our holiness greatly pleases the Father. This is why, in establishing the Law with the children of Israel, God repeatedly told Moses, "Speak to the entire assembly of Israel and say to them: 'Be holy because I, the LORD your God, am holy'" (Leviticus 19:2, 11:44-45).

Similar to the fenced school playground, the covenant of marriage is a place of complete safety. Because God is holy and He demands nothing but holiness from us as individuals, we can conclude that He longs for holiness in our marriages as well. The writer of Hebrews states it like this: "Marriage should be honored by all, and the marriage bed kept pure, for God will judge the adulterer and all the sexually immoral" (Hebrews 13:4).

We agree with Corrie ten Boom's statement that there is no safer place than in the center of the will of God. The protective boundaries of marriage were established long ago by God and demonstrated in the original marriage in the garden of Eden (Genesis 2). The foundations of God's fences were laid with His unchanging love for us, and the structure of these barriers was erected using wisdom and understanding. They are built of eternally unchanging truth, and they demonstrate, both to the world and to us, the absolute goodness of God. They were not laid because God didn't want us to have fun. The boundaries were erected so we could have the most fun possible in the context of marriage. Remember, holy is fun!

A marriage truly connected to the holiness of God is an amazing thing. In this kind of relationship we can let down all our defenses and just *be* instead of always *doing* and trying to perform. We fulfill the destiny God created us to enjoy as we walk in the holiness of marriage. In this place all is freely shared and no barrier exists between husband and wife. There is no fear about what the other person might think, nor is there any doubt concerning the motivations of each other's actions. In God's playground called marriage, we are encouraged to love deeply and freely, to laugh and to play, without fear of the dangers that lie outside of these God-ordained boundaries.

There has been no restraint in the Father's demonstration of love to us through the giving of Jesus. "For God so loved the world that he gave his one and only Son, that whoever believes in him shall not perish but have eternal life" (John 3:16). Paul asks, "He who did not spare his own Son, but gave him up for us all—how will he not also, along with him, graciously give us all things?" (Romans 8:32).

Likewise, He urges us in marriage to have no restraint as we verbalize and act out our love for each other. When we walk in the boundaries God has given us for marriage, there is nothing that is held back in the mutual giving of love between husband and wife.

A Ticklish Situation

We love an amazing couple in Uganda who beautifully demonstrate this life of holiness and purity before God. These two serve as pastors at a huge church located in the largest slum in Kampala. The entire church is vibrant and alive even though the members are among the poorest of the poor. Every day the leaders in this church hear of terrible needs among their church members. Without relating to our big, supernatural God, it would be easy for the pastors to be overwhelmed and discouraged. They know it is vital that they keep the oil of the Spirit in their lamps (Matthew 25).

Pastor James (not his real name) came to us after a conference where we were teaching about supernatural marriage. With not a little embarrassment, he confessed to us that passion for his wife was stirred whenever they worshipped together at home. They knew that prayer and worship fueled their hearts, enabling them to give to the church day in and day out. They loved adoring God together in the privacy of their home. They wanted to walk in purity. But they were both concerned that becoming amorous during worship at home was dishonoring or unpleasing to God.

Holy Moses, no! Of course worship is never to be used as a tool to promote sex. Yet God *delights* in our enjoying each other. He wants you to have passion for your marriage partner. This does not take away from the passion we have for Him. Enjoying each other in marriage and purity actually *enhances* our intimacy with God.

This might be a good time for you to put down this book and pick up *the* Book. Turn to the Song of Solomon (some Bible versions call it the Song of Songs). Read it with your eyes and heart open to hear the passion and love inspired by the Lover of your soul.

What Is Holiness?

What exactly *is* holiness? Let's begin answering that question by learning more about what it means to be holy.

Several times in the book of Leviticus God says to "be holy as I am holy" (11:44). How can wives and husbands be holy? It is encouraging to remember that this is the same God who said, "Let there be light," and through His word it became a reality. The command to be holy implies an expectation from God, but also the anticipation that His word will make it happen. Jesus is "the word" (John 1:14) through which the Father's decree of holiness can be fulfilled.

Being holy is to be separate from the ordinary, unattached to the profane. To become holy we must meet and join with God. This is what Moses did at the burning bush (Exodus 3) and what the high priest did once a year by entering the holy of holies in the tabernacle (Leviticus 16). It is what we can do by receiving the Holy Spirit of God and entering His presence through worship. The Spirit connects us to the one who defines holiness, He who is perfect in goodness and righteousness. We become holy through the influence of God's character and love—inner transformation of our hearts and souls. We can become holy, dedicated to God.

What Is Purity?

"The conduct of the pure is upright" (Proverbs 21:8). Being pure implies guiltless, blameless, innocent behavior. Purity is the natural outflow of a heart pursuing holiness. One is never present without the other. The two go hand in hand. David wrote, "Who may ascend the hill of the LORD? Who may stand in his holy place? He who has clean hands and a pure heart" (Psalm 24:3–4).

Through transformation by God's Holy Spirit, we become more holy and our behavior becomes more pure. Paul called Timothy to exhibit a lifestyle of purity to set an example for other believers (1 Timothy 4:12). We are also called to live with our mates in an atmosphere marked by purity. There is no more enjoyable and satisfying place to be.

Say Yes to Him

God's desire for intimacy with us is beautifully described in the Song of Solomon. The Bridegroom, Jesus, speaks to the church as His bride: "You have ravished my heart, my sister, my bride;

you have ravished my heart with a glance of your eyes, with one jewel of your necklace" (Song of Solomon 4:9 NRSV). Imagine how a life full of loving obedience could develop the intimate romance Jesus desires to have with each one of us as part of His bride. Each move we make toward the Lover of our souls strengthens the shared bond of love. Every time we say yes to Him, His tender heart is ravished again.

If we live in impurity, God's passionate love for us remains the same; however, the intimacy of our relationship with Him will change. This is not a vengeful response on God's part, but the natural result of our thoughts and actions that are in opposition to His holiness. God is completely holy; if we are to be in Him and He is to be in us, as Jesus declared (John 17:21), we must honestly pursue holiness. Without holiness, the writer of Hebrews says, "No one will see the Lord" (12:14). Jesus said something similar when He said a pure heart is a prerequisite to seeing God: "Blessed are the pure in heart, for they will see God" (Matthew 5:8).

By one sacrifice on the cross, Jesus has made all who are saved positionally perfect. He also continues to make them holy in all their conduct. "By one sacrifice he has made perfect forever those who are being made holy" (Hebrews 10:14). We are led into holiness through the presence of the Holy Spirit within us. The Spirit places God's laws in our hearts and writes them in our minds (Hebrews 10:16).

The indwelling Spirit of God shows us the way we should go just as He led the Israelites with the cloud by day and the fire by night (Deuteronomy 1:33). Following the leading of the Spirit is not difficult, as is often thought to be the case. The glory of God passing before us makes the way of the righteous level and smooth (Isaiah 26:7). When we are faithful with a small degree of God's intimate presence, He gives us more—similar to what was done in the parable of the talents (Matthew 25:28–29). As we continue to increase in our connectedness with God through the Holy Spirit, we are permanently changed.

Pursuing Purity

We have a tendency to undervalue the importance of purity and overestimate the difficulty in achieving it. Purity is worthy of passionate pursuit by all believers. We cannot become holy with our own effort. Holiness can only be achieved by the Spirit of God producing His attributes in our lives. Yet when our bodies are earthly temples that house the actual presence of God's Holy Spirit, we are effortlessly drawn into living lives that are holy. God's glory transforms us to become more and more holy because that is His nature.

It is truly a joy to live a pure life before the Lord. We demonstrate how much we value God's free gift of love by lovingly returning it to Him through faithful obedience. Jesus said, "If anyone loves me, he will obey my teaching. My Father will love him, and we will come to him and make our home with him" (John 14:23).

God's plan for purity is extremely simple, yet wise and effective. Because "God is love" (1 John 4:8), we receive His love through experiencing His presence. God's love and His presence are permanently linked together. We respond to God's love by loving Him in return. "We love because he first loved us," John writes (1 John 4:19). And as Jesus said in John 14:23, we demonstrate our love for God by voluntary obedience. When we lovingly obey the one who calls us to be holy (Leviticus 11:45), God changes us to become more like Himself. What occurs is not theology or semantics. Through transformation by God we become more pure in our hearts and holy in His sight.

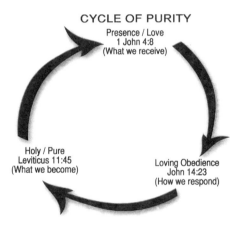

CYCLE OF PURITY

Presence / Love
1 John 4:8
(What we receive)

Holy / Pure
Leviticus 11:45
(What we become)

Loving Obedience
John 14:23
(How we respond)

This cycle of purity can become self-perpetuating and never ending. Like a snowball on a mountainside, it gains momentum and continually builds upon itself. As we become holy, God will more freely share His presence with us. We respond to the increase in His loving presence with more consistent willful obedience. When we are more faithful to God's leading,

He increases our level of purity. We become holy to the Lord and an attractive resting place for the manifest glory of Holy God. The importance of this eternally revolving cycle cannot be overstated. If we are to fulfill the purposes for which we were created, it is essential that we become holy and reflect His character in our lives.

Purity for a Lifetime

Purity before God is regularly taught to young men and women during their courtship years. Unfortunately, this teaching is often ignored when it comes to actual practice. Participation in sexual sin at any age results in harmful ripples that cause a degree of personal and relational injury that can persist throughout life. There is good reason Paul instructs us, "Among you there must not be even a hint of sexual immorality, or of any kind of impurity…because these are improper for God's holy people" (Ephesians 5:3). He also writes to the church in Corinth with the warning, "Flee from sexual immorality" (1 Corinthians 6:18). These are strong words due to the extreme damage caused by every sexual relationship outside of marriage.

Certainly God's grace is sufficient to limit the harm that is done when people participate in these sins, and there is "no condemnation for those who are in Christ Jesus" (Romans 8:1). Still, as David learned after his sin with Bathsheba, participation with sin causes serious injury to those involved, and it results in far-reaching negative consequences (2 Samuel 12:9–14).

Although we tend to relax our attention to this matter after marriage vows are taken, the importance of complete purity does not decrease in the least. The convenience and availability of sexual gratification with a marital partner does not alter patterns of self-centeredness, rebellion, and lust, which may have been present for years before the wedding. If satan has been successful in drawing a couple into sinful behavior prior to marriage, it is certain his efforts to destroy their lives will not stop simply because marital vows have been spoken, even when spoken with real commitment.

Sexual purity in marriage is much more than avoiding the physical act of adultery. Our sexual interest must be completely directed toward our own spouses if we are to walk in righteousness and holiness before the Lord. This focus is achieved only by submitting full control of our thoughts, plans, recreational activities, entertainment options, and relationships to the Holy Spirit. Our imaginations must also be completely under the lordship of Jesus. Even during sexual relations within marriage, our imaginations can drift into impurity and wickedness. Any form of persistent impurity can destroy close connectedness with God and eventually devastate the physical and emotional intimacies so vital to marriage.

Source of Hope

Recognition of sinful behavior can actually be a source of hope. Our desire to become more holy can be renewed by the realization that we have not yet reached perfection. The confession of our sins to others, often including our spouses, is required if God is to forgive our sins and purify us from all unrighteousness. John wrote, "If we claim to be without sin, we deceive ourselves and the truth is not in us. If we confess our sins, he is faithful and just and will forgive us our sins and purify us from all unrighteousness" (1 John 1:8–9). The supernatural love of God can draw us into faithful obedience, honoring His complete lordship over our lives.

After being confronted by Nathan the prophet, David confessed his sin and humbled himself before God (2 Samuel 12:16). He again walked in obedience before the Lord, fulfilling the ultimate destiny for which he was created. Regardless of what we have done, God is capable of transforming us into the holy priests we were created to be (1 Peter 2:5). David's destiny wasn't thwarted because he fell in a moment of weakness. No, God still used all things together for good to fulfill His purpose in David's life, even extending blessing through David's descendants to us today.

Marriage Garden

As holy priests of a holy God, we are called to do our part in accomplishing the plan of holy matrimony. Within each of us is immense capability to receive and give supernatural love. Solomon compares marital relationships, as well as our relationships with God, to a magnificent garden filled with every imaginable visual, tactile, and olfactory pleasure.

Solomon wrote:

You are a garden locked up, my sister, my bride; you are a spring enclosed, a sealed fountain. Your plants are an orchard of pomegranates with choice fruits, with henna and nard, nard and saffron, calamus and cinnamon, with every kind of incense tree, with myrrh and aloes and all the finest spices. You are a garden fountain, a well of flowing water streaming down from Lebanon (Song of Solomon 4:12–15).

The garden fountain and the well of flowing water of verse 15 represent the streams of living water Jesus later said would flow out of us (John 7:38). A believing spouse brings this same living water to the garden of marriage. In supernatural marriage, the presence of the true and living God is carried within the relationship. The life-giving water of the Spirit springs forth forever from the perfect love of God. With a never-ending supply of life pouring into the garden, its potential for growth is limitless.

The water streaming down from Lebanon into Israel was delightfully unpolluted. Similarly, every spouse in intimate communion with God brings into the relationship pure "water welling up to eternal life" (John 4:14). This garden is gloriously beautiful because it is constantly supplied with pure water for vitality and growth.

Supernatural marriage is much like the magnificent garden described in the Song of Solomon. When both partners earnestly pursue intimacy with God and with each other, their relationship can be filled with astounding beauty through the continual presence of God Himself. When they are in God and God is in them, their marital garden becomes a modern reiteration of the idyllic oneness enjoyed by Adam and Eve in the garden of Eden. If both spouses truly seek first the kingdom of God and His righteousness, all the things that are needed for their life and ministry together will be given to them as well (Matthew 6:33).

Innocence

Isn't it fun to watch children's faces? Kids are transparent. We are never left to guess if they are happy, sad, or excited. Their faces readily let us know what they are feeling. And is there anything more precious than a child's face as she sleeps? At times when our sons were little we would tiptoe into their rooms just to watch them for a moment—innocent, pure, and sweet.

In supernatural marriage we get to enjoy this innocence with our mates. We can afford the luxury of being real, of being open and vulnerable, exposing our hearts to our lover and our God. We are free, and we are safe to be exactly who we are without pretense. This is holiness.

7 Secrets Suggestion

Holy really is fun. Being pure before the Lord is wonderful, but it requires action. Is there a novel you need to burn? A movie you should destroy? "Clean house" together as a celebration honoring the Lord.

SECRET 7: ROMANCE

Romance is not something turned on after the kids are in bed. It is a lifestyle based on deep intimacy with each other and with God. The Lover of your soul teaches you how to be the greatest lover for your mate.

Maybe you've heard the saying that variety is the spice of life. This certainly holds true in romance! It is like fireworks—sometimes sparklers, sometimes firecrackers, and occasionally a really big fireworks show. Not every day is the Fourth of July, but we can enjoy sparklers any time we wish.

Romance is not something we turn on only after the kids are in bed. It is a lifestyle of sweet, beautiful sparklers, based on deep intimacy with each other and with God. The Lover of our souls nudges us to know when to shoot off bottle rockets and Roman candles. And sometimes He lets us know it's a great time for a big fireworks display with all the loud booms that make the ground shake and bright colors that leave us in awe.

Romance is the seventh secret of a supernatural marriage. It will provide you and your mate with fond memories for a lifetime. Let the fireworks begin!

An Extreme Romantic

God is unquestionably an extreme romantic. Soon after speaking life into Adam, God expressed awareness of man's need for emotional and physical intimacy with another person he could love. God said, "It is not good for the man to be alone" (Genesis 2:18). Through forming Eve from Adam's rib, our Father produced the essential second half of the first romantic relationship. These two individuals, now united as one, became the original prototype for all human romance and marriages for ages to come.

The setting for this love relationship was idyllic—a man and a woman in a magnificent physical environment, surrounded by the perfect love of God. He would stroll with them in the cool of the day. No one since that time has had the same type of relationship with the Father, save Jesus Himself. There was no sin to separate them from God. They felt at home in God's presence because that is where they were created to be. They were also naked "and they felt no shame" (Genesis 2:25), totally familiar with each other and intimately connected to the one who provided everything they needed.

Surrender

God's desire is that you willingly submit every aspect of who you are to Him, the perfect Lover of your soul. In marriage you symbolically act out this submission to Him every time you surrender your heart, will, or body to your mate. In supernatural marriage this yielding to your partner's needs and desires occurs on a regular basis. It is led by the Spirit of Christ and is done out of reverence for Him. This is one reason Paul, in the context of marriage, wrote, "Submit to one another out of reverence for Christ" (Ephesians 5:21). Hmm. Does this remind you of the first of the 7 secrets—lordship?

If Jesus' lordship is to be complete, it is necessary for you to fully submit your body to Him. This is taught regularly to young men and women during courtship years, in the hope they will remain pure in their physical relationships. However, lordship of your body is no less significant after marriage than before. During every part of life your body is meant for the Lord (1 Corinthians 6:13). When you have ears to hear what the Spirit speaks and consistently obey what you have heard, you will do the things with your physical body that most honor and glorify God. He will lead you into the very best ways to bless your marital partner through romance and sexual intimacy.

Your body is not your own. It belongs to God. Paul wrote to the Corinthians in his first letter, "Do you not know that your body is a temple of the Holy Spirit, who is in you, whom you have received from God? You are not your own; you were bought at a price. Therefore honor God with your body" (1 Corinthians 6:19–20). Not only does your body belong to God, but He has given it to your spouse. In fact, Paul goes on to talk about this not too much later in the same letter, giving some wisdom about marriage. He said:

> The husband should fulfill his marital duty to his wife, and likewise the wife to her husband. The wife's body does not belong to her alone but also to her husband. In the same way, the husband's body does not belong to him alone but also to his wife. Do not deprive each other except by mutual consent and for a time, so that you may devote yourselves to prayer. (1 Corinthians 7:3–6)

God uses your body as a powerful tool through which both His and your love can be beautifully demonstrated to your partner. Even the love you think is yours originated within the heart of God. In supernatural marriage His perfect love flows through each partner to the other, without restriction or pause.

The pure and holy love of the Father is the eternally flowing wellspring of life, the ultimate source of everything needed to establish and maintain spiritual, emotional, and physical oneness in marriage. One aspect of the way love is shown is through sexual intimacy. But before we get into sexual intimacy, it is valuable to discuss the need for emotional intimacy. Before a spouse feels connected in a sexual way, there is a great need to connect on an emotional, romantic level.

Everyday Romance

The most important romantic events leading to successful sexual relations are those that occur hours, days, or even years earlier. These are the experiences that establish closeness and bonding between the marriage partners. They are indispensible in maintaining long-term emotional intimacy.

A marriage that exhibits reliable and enjoyable everyday romance is well equipped to proceed smoothly into sexual intimacy. However, a marriage based on sexuality alone is ill prepared for building a loving and trusting long-term relationship. This is one reason God commands us to abstain from sex prior to marriage. Although all aspects of sexuality become freely available to spouses in marriage, the less physical, even nonsexual forms of romance continue to be extremely important and really fun!

The key to effective everyday romance is for each partner to honestly and consistently express love to the other in ways that can be received. The love communicated must be both selfless *(agape)* and lifelong *(phileo)*. Daily expressions of love might encourage a spouse toward sexual intimacy. However, the primary purpose of regular romantic gestures is to convey love, acceptance, and genuine interest in fulfilling the needs of your spouse. It must not be intended or perceived as manipulation of any kind. Manipulation is dangerous, even deadly, to romance.

Do you often express warm thoughts to your spouse? Words that bring unity and enhance intimacy? A few of the sentiments we express are:

"I like you."

"I love you."

"I enjoy you."

"I care for you."

"I appreciate you."

"I desire to be with you."

"You are very special to me."

These thoughts can be conveyed in a number of ways Regardless of the means, the communication of these thoughts transmits the messages of love and tenderness that are crucial to both emotional and physical intimacy in marriage.

It is essential to be affectionate and flirty with your spouse on a regular basis, not only when you are in the mood for sex. There is great enjoyment and pleasure in romantically expressing love and tenderness without immediate plans to progress further in making love. It is particularly good for the husband to plan ahead of time that his advances will not physically go beyond a certain point that hour, or perhaps that day. This intentional delay of gratification communicates to his wife that expressing pure love to her is his ultimate goal not having sex.

Tips for Romance

Allow us to share with you a few tips we have found to be fun in enhancing romance:

- Be physically near each other whenever possible.
- Speak honest, complimentary words about your spouse to others. Do this both with and without him or her being present.

- God loves it when you have a thankful heart, and your spouse will too! Express thanks often concerning both big and little things.
- When separated in a crowd, periodically acknowledge each other's presence using eye contact and a smile, brief verbal communication, or even a hint of a kiss passed through the air, with no physical contact. We learned this years ago from our pet parakeet who blew us kisses from across the room.
- Briefly touch as you pass each other, whether alone, in a group, or swimming at the community pool.
- Make short phone calls to each other while at work, just long enough to say, "I love you," or, "I miss you massively."
- Loving or flirty text messages can be extremely fun. Be bold, but be wise.
- Write capital letters that symbolize tender thoughts on each other's hands or backs with your fingers. (We use ILYVVVM! to say, "I love you very, very, very much!")
- Write love notes on napkins placed in sack lunches taken to work. It is amazing what can be effectively communicated to a spouse through these words, discreetly kept from the eyes of coworkers.
- Mail "Thank You" or "I Love You" cards to each other to be delivered at home or at work.
- Send flowers or bring home small gifts for no reason other than to communicate how special your spouse is to you.

- Play romantic games together. For example, have code words that can be spoken in public places with which you can easily communicate private and intimate thoughts to each other.
- Reminisce regularly about past fun and romantic experiences together.
- Plan a trip for your spouse to a surprise destination celebrating a big birthday or other special event. The extravagance of the trip is not the point. What is crucial is demonstrating love in the planning and forethought. Design the trip to include ample couple time.
- Flirt frequently. Be creative. It's fun!
- Holding hands is really nice also. You can do it almost anywhere without restriction or embarrassment. We did a lot of this on our first date and have continued to enjoy it frequently ever since.
- Sensuously share a large chocolate truffle.
- Exercise with each other regularly, even if it is only walking a mile together while talking.
- Eat as many meals together as possible. It is very helpful to leave the television off. Visit about significant events of the day and try to listen at least as much as you talk.
- Establish a bedtime routine and follow it whenever able. We enjoy cuddling together on the sofa each night while we read Scripture to each other. Then we pray together for whatever length of time seems right before falling asleep.

- Each night, through words and touch, express love to each other one last time before going to sleep. This can be done even with just a sensual, sexy touch. Being reminded that you are one with each other and one with God, you will rest peacefully through the night.

Why Not Be Nice?

For years Linda and I have had an expression one of us will say to the other when we're being thanked for doing something exceptionally sweet. We commonly respond with "Why *not* be nice?" At the moment it is said mostly in fun, but being nice is seriously important in the pursuit of passion. Kindness and gentleness are critical in maintaining the romantic ambiance of a close relationship. Every word that is spoken can be enveloped in *agape l*ove. Try it. You'll like it.

Knowing how to endearingly relate to your mate is not difficult. Jesus condensed the message of all Scripture into one phrase we refer to as "the Golden Rule." He said, "So in everything, *do to others what you would have them do to you,* for this sums up the Law and the Prophets" (Matthew 7:12, emphasis added). This simple instruction can transform the way a wife and husband relate to each other. When you treat your lover the way you would like to be treated, the romantic and sexual environment of your marriage will improve.

Nothing is more romantic than persistently pursuing and doing things that bless the one you love. If you have ears to hear what the Spirit says (Revelation 3:22), God will lead you to know where, when, and how to best show love to your partner. And who knows? You might enjoy some fabulous fireworks along the way.

Great Sex

God really likes sex. In fact, it was His idea from the beginning. It is His good pleasure when great sex brings you pleasure. He wants you to experience lovemaking that is beyond satisfying. God wants sex to knock your socks off!

Proverbs 30 refers to sexual intimacy as something that cannot be fully understood. Agur wrote, "There are three things that are too amazing for me, four that I do not understand: the way of an eagle in the sky, the way of a snake on a rock, the way of a ship on the high seas, and the way of a man with a maiden" (Proverbs 30:18–19). We agree with Agur. Sex enjoyed within the covenant of marriage is meant to be amazing. Breathtaking. Beautiful.

As with other areas in supernatural marriage, it is imperative to not settle for mediocrity in lovemaking. God created our bodies to enjoy sexual play in ways that are beyond description. At times it can be absolutely astonishing. Do not accept "pretty good" as the ultimate goal for your sexual intimacy. Make the effort to optimize this very pleasurable aspect of marriage. God places no limit on the bliss that can be experienced together during sexual encounters, the Fourth of July kind of fireworks display. Spend a lifetime with your mate pursuing the best ways to enjoy this indescribably delicious gift from heaven.

Always, Yes Always

The Holy Spirit desires to be helpful in every aspect of life, including the sexual encounters of your marriage. In the Old Testament God told Joshua, "As I was with Moses, so I will be with you; I will never leave you nor forsake you" (Joshua 1:5). The gospel of Matthew ends with Jesus encouraging His disciples with the words "Surely I am with you always, to the very end of the age" (Matthew 28:20).

Does God withdraw His holy presence during the times you are passionately involved in sexual relations within the covenant of marriage? No! When you and your mate join together, He is there with you (Matthew 18:20). The presence of God is no less real during sexual play than at any other time in your life. Remember, He created sex. He loves it when we love each other.

Freedom—Even to Say No

Where the Spirit of the Lord is, there is freedom (2 Corinthians 3:17). To reach the highest levels of sexual expression, both you and your partner must be free. God enables you to be extravagant, intimate lovers. Are there limits to sexual freedom? Of course there are. Are you required to do everything your partner desires? You are not.

There are times when you and your mate will have different opinions about what is desirable and enjoyable within the realm of sexual play. It is crucial to say no to an activity that might be uncomfortable, unpleasant, or possibly unwise. In these instances it is helpful if the no can be spoken in a kind way that leaves hope for the trying of other creative ideas in the future. When resistance to any sexual activity is perceived to be coming from your partner, it is vital that it be stopped or delayed unless receptivity is established.

Consider a small child being encouraged to jump from a diving board to his father, who is patiently waiting in the deep water below. It could emotionally injure the child to be forced off the end of the board. Eventually, the jump is made voluntarily, leading to a lifetime of enjoying a wonderful form of recreation. Similarly, each spouse should coax the other into discovering new ways to relax and have fun together, but should never push the other into any form of physical intimacy.

Pleasing Your Mate

Sexual play within marriage has many purposes, including procreation, expression of love, physical demonstration of oneness, mutually shared pleasure, emotional release, stress relief, as well as physical satisfaction. Every one of these purposes is optimized when your primary goal in sexual play is that your spouse fully enjoys everything that is done. This is consistent with Paul's command in Philippians 2 where he wrote, "Do nothing out of selfish ambition or vain conceit, but in humility consider others better than yourselves. Each of you should look not only to your own interests, but also to the interests of others" (3–4). Mutual selflessness is key to sexual fulfillment.

A frequent challenge to selflessness is when husbands and wives have different desires as to the frequency of their sexual encounters. It is rare that spouses' opinions in this area match, though they often become closer to the same after a decade or two of marriage. The basis of this discrepancy is not so much psychological as it is physical. Often, though not always, the higher-frequency spouse is the man.

Husbands are, in general, quite predictable. After an orgasm it is typical for a man's libido to markedly decrease and then slowly build again over the next three to five days. This pattern is so common and predictable that it has led to the establishment of marital laws. For example, there is a law currently in effect in Afghanistan that allows husbands to demand sex with their wives every four days.[5] The fact that such a law would even be considered clearly shows that the timing of peak interest in sex is often quite different in men and women.

The variation of libido in women is harder to predict than in men. It tends to be much more complex and is often related to the hormonal changes of the monthly menstrual cycle. It can be very difficult, particularly during the first years of marriage, for a husband or wife to understand each other's sexual desires and needs. It is extremely helpful for each to recognize that the other's pattern of sexual interest is built into them by God with wisdom and purpose. Although the peaks of desire may not always mesh

---

5   This law was in effect as of 6/1/14 per Wikipedia: http://en.wikipedia.org/wiki/Shia_Family_Law. Also see the BBC article dated 8/16/09: http://news.bbc.co.uk/2/hi/8204207.stm.

well, they should be dealt with through gentleness, patience, and love—by both the higher- and the lower-frequency spouse.

Correct timing can make all the difference in a woman's ability to respond and fully enjoy sex. Patience is one of the fruits of the Spirit that God places in our hearts (Galatians 5:22), and wisdom is given to us directly by God (Proverbs 1:6). When a man is patient, allowing wisdom to tell him when and how to pursue intimacy with his wife, the results are beyond amazing. It is said in real estate that the three most important things are location, location, and location. Aside from the presence of true *agape* love in a marriage, the three most critical factors in shared sexual satisfaction are timing, timing, and timing.

On any given day a man may be amorous while his wife is not. This means neither that his libido is inappropriately high nor that hers is inadequate. Similarly, it is normal that on some days the woman might be more interested in sex than her husband. Some asymmetry in the sexual desires of marital partners is nearly always present. Working through this difference may seem at times to be an insurmountable challenge. In truth, God designed the sexual libidos of men and women with perfect wisdom and purpose. This difference in wives and husbands presents them both with a tremendous opportunity to show love by adapting to each other's needs.

Satisfying Sex

Paul writes, "I want you to be wise about what is good, and innocent about what is evil." (Romans 16:19). It is vital for us to be wise throughout life concerning the best ways to experience physical intimacy. Sexuality within marriage is created by God and is meant to be fantastic. Through sex you can participate in the creation of new life, make memories by sharing love for each other, and strengthen the marital union by freely giving and receiving intense pleasure. Being good at sex requires learning how to physically please your partner with joy and purity of heart. It is wise to be good at things that really matter.

Although quite important, sexual relations are not the primary focus of the healthiest marriages. There are situations in which physical intimacy is impossible, yet the marital union remains strong. Still, for most couples, a joint level of satisfaction with physical intimacy is a sensitive and important indicator for the well-being of their relationship as a whole. Both should be pleased that their sexual needs are adequately met, while at the same time each experiences great joy in knowing his or her partner is sexually content.

It is valuable for you to regularly communicate with your partner concerning his or her level of sexual contentment. Decreasing satisfaction with any aspect of marriage is best discussed when first noticed. You are blessed when you find wisdom and gain understanding (Proverbs 3:13), both of which are supplied by God. Wisdom allows you to identify problems, while understanding teaches you how to deal with them. When the source of difficulty is discovered and healed, every part of the marital relationship benefits.

Satisfying sex provides remarkable strength and stability

for marriage. It helps both partners to maintain purity, remain faithful to God, and keep their marriage vows. There are many paths to gratifying physical intimacy. Be adventurous! Making love is meant to be full of discovery.

Sensual Tips

Here are a few tips for sensual thinking and behaving that will make your mate feel both loved and desired. As you read through these, let them spark your imagination. We suggest you implement some of them soon, even tonight.

- Don't take lovemaking too seriously. Laugh and act silly. Fully enjoy your most intimate friend. This is play, not work!
- Go to bed together and wake up together as often as possible. Make this your normal and most desired routine.
- Buy sexy underwear and use them. (And yes, throw away some of the old, comfy ones.)
- Pay attention to personal hygiene. The cleaner, the better!
- Reminisce about particularly special sexual times together as you pursue the making of memories for the future.
- Coax, but never push your partner toward intimacy.
- Visual flirting is fun, even in a crowd. Catch each other's eyes with a prolonged gaze that clearly communicates your thoughts.

- Touch each other frequently in nonsexual ways. Gradually ramp up the intimacy of the touches when a receptive response is noticed.
- Don't be in a hurry. Take your time and enjoy the process.
- Ask questions like "Does this feel good?" or "What would feel even better?"
- Avoid getting into ruts. Variety really is the spice of life. Use your God-given creativity to vary the time, location, and ambiance of sexual play.
- Occasionally try new positions and new ways of pleasuring each other.
- Say no when necessary, but always with love and hope so your spouse is not turned off for creativity in future intimacy.
- Surprise your lover from time to time with something completely unexpected.
- Discover a new way to enjoy the great outdoors.
- Never fear being ridiculous. You might miss experiencing something that is really fun.
- It is all right to be shy, but be sure your wishes are made known. When you feel sexual desire, communicate this in a way that you are confident your partner will understand. Do not allow your spouse to miss the opportunity to enjoy you.

As you experiment in lovemaking, concentrate on your partner's needs and desires above your own. There are days when one of you might have very little sexual desire. On those days, share love in alternative ways—talking, less sexual touching, acts of service, spending time together. Patience and self-control are fruits of the Spirit. Both qualities are of great value in the pursuit of sexual intimacy. God will supply these virtues to those who are wise enough to ask for them. They will lead you into a better understanding of the best times, places, and ways to enjoy sex in your marriage.

If you want to know what is pleasing to your spouse, just ask. But remember, it may be difficult for him or her to answer such a direct question. It is always a good idea to ask the Holy Spirit what to do in any situation. God has given you ears to hear what the Spirit is saying to you about your marriage and the best way to pursue sexual intimacy. All you have to do is ask and listen. He will tell you exactly what you need to know. Wow! He really is the all-wise God!

Fireworks Display

Romantic fireworks are great! We like holding sparklers and writing "ILY" or our first initials in the air. But although sparklers are nice, we really love bigger fireworks. Sometimes Dan holds a punk in his hand to light the firecrackers; at other times Linda holds it. Regardless of who initiates, we have a delightful time watching the colors explode.

Then there are those delicious occasions when the fireworks show is magnificent. Each burst of the rocket rains down brilliant, sparkling colors that delight our senses. Those moments we celebrate and savor.

Sexual play is a romantic celebration. It is a glorious way to enjoy the abundant life of supernatural marriage. Play often. Play with enthusiasm. Play with passion. Play with joy. Play!

7 Secrets Suggestion

Grab a blanket, a picnic basket, and your mate. Linger over a simple meal as you have fun recalling your special fireworks displays. These memories will surely entice you to want more.

MAN + WOMAN + HOLY SPIRIT = SUPERNATURAL MARRIAGE

There was a sweet three-year-old boy in a children's Bible class Linda taught one year. The holy week of Easter came and a big Easter egg hunt was provided for all the children. Each of the kids delighted in running around the grassy area looking for eggs. But one little guy did something very unusual. He skipped past eggs of any color other than blue. His basket was filled with only blue eggs. When asked about this curious way of gathering the eggs, he simply replied, "My favorite color is blue."

This true story reminds us of one found in Matthew 13:44. "The kingdom of heaven is like treasure hidden in a field. When a man found it, he hid it again, and then in his joy went and sold all he had and bought that field." The hidden treasures God has for us, His children, are many. But dear friend, we submit to you that supernatural marriage is one of the very special treasures. Do not be swayed by eggs of a different color. Sell everything you have and buy this field!

Supernatural marriage is neither the impossible dream nor an unreachable star. It is not reserved for the fortunate few. It is a kingdom treasure available to all whom God calls into holy matrimony. This heavenly kind of marital relationship is not only available for someone else. Supernatural marriage is available for you.

7 Secrets Released

The 7 secrets—lordship, passion, presence, power, transformation, holiness, and romance—can all be used to bless marriages, even when limited to the natural realm. Yes, you can have a good marriage through commitment and effort alone. But good is not the best. You and your mate were created for much more. The ultimate marriage, the one that astounds you both with joy-filled satisfaction, can be experienced exclusively in the supernatural realm. The Holy Spirit is the catalyst that releases all 7 secrets to their fullest possible expression. Only the Spirit of God can take you where you really want to go.

The marriage you thirst for, the supernatural marriage you crave, will not be enjoyed if you cling to the wisdom and ways of this natural world. God has begun a good work in you and He will carry it on to completion (Philippians 1:6). God is a supernatural being whose power is shown in His supernatural realm. "He performs wonders that cannot be fathomed, miracles that cannot be counted" (Job 9:10).

Supernatural marriage is one of God's most magnificent miracles. In it He combines flesh and spirit, natural and supernatural, the perfect lover and the perfectly loved. Nothing is held back and nothing is left out. The glory of the Creator is seen in that which He gloriously created. It is a kingdom treasure that transcends the borders of nations and the limitations of this world. Cultural variations do not alter the eternal truths of God and His Word. His presence, passion, and power are available to every spouse in every civilization on earth. Supernatural marriage is filled with heaven's glory in Beijing just as it is in Auckland, Nairobi, Santiago, Dallas, Vijayawada, and Berlin.

The Key

Remember the treasure chest from Dan's dream we told you about in the opening chapter? Supernatural marriage is a treasure that has been hidden for you to find. The key to the treasure chest, childlikeness, has been placed in your hand. The 7 Secrets have been revealed. Are you willing to use the key and put the secrets into action? Dare you throw off whatever has been entangling you so you can joyfully pursue this field?

Jesus calls us to become like little children (Matthew 18:3). Part of this change is accepting the value of naïveté. We need to be just naïve enough to believe that God will do what He says. He really will provide everything you need for life and godliness (2 Peter 1:3). Do you trust that He wants to do this? Do you believe that He can?

You have dreamed of having a wonderful marriage. You crave

to see the glory of His plan. God Himself has placed this desire within you. Only the Holy Spirit can propel your marriage into the place both you and He desire for it to be. God's secret treasure is being revealed in our day—waiting to be discovered by you and your mate. Are you ready to discover it?

> The secret things belong to the LORD our God, but the things revealed belong to us and to our children forever.
> Deuteronomy 29:29

Mighty River

Years ago, Dan had a powerful dream that has helped define both our marriage and our ministry. The dream consisted of a short, action-packed scene in which we were floating on our backs in a large, beautiful river—laughing and splashing in the water as the current effortlessly took us wherever the river might go. With laughter and great joy we invited every person standing on the shore to jump into the river, joining us in our blissful and exuberant journey together.

Dan can see the dream as clearly today as the first night he saw it.

Is there anything in the refreshing river of God's Spirit you don't want? It is the constant source of everything we need. This supernatural river flows with the wisdom of heaven, transcendent peace, and love, bringing complete satisfaction. The Holy Spirit is the wellspring of abundant life for all who are willing to allow this mighty river of God to carry them on to their destiny.

If your heart's desire is to fully satisfy God's plan for you in marriage, you must be in the channel of this rapidly flowing river. You can only experience the ultimate intimacy God designed to be in marriage through intimate communion with the one who created it. We invite you, with passion in our hearts and smiles on our faces, to join us in the astounding joy of Spirit-led intimacy that leads to supernatural marriage.

7 Secrets Suggestion

You and your marriage can be blessed forever in the eternal, supernatural realm of heaven. Ask God to reposition you and your marriage, allowing Him to place both in the center of this mighty river, flowing with His perfect love. You will never regret diving into Him!

HOW TO LIVE WHEN UNEQUALLY YOKED

W e recently spent an evening talking and praying with a woman we will call Laura to protect her identity. For years she has been committed to obediently following Jesus with her whole heart. Her faith in God is real and her love for Him is deep. Laura is a serious and mature believer.

The primary frustration in Laura's life is that her husband is a nominal Christian who is content to stay the way he is. He likes to be with Laura and resents the time she spends away from him while participating in worship, Bible study, prayer, and ministry. The most important and enjoyable part of Laura's life is the time she spends closely connecting with God. Yet she cannot talk about this with her husband because doing so makes him annoyed and even angry.

Long ago the powers of darkness erected a spiritual wall between Laura and her husband. These two individuals are one flesh in marriage, but they see life from the perspectives of two different kingdoms. Laura and her husband hold diverging beliefs as to what is ultimately of true value in their lives. With time the wall between them has become so thick that it seems impenetrable to the sharing of healthy emotions or the communication of love.

Laura had become extremely discouraged and was at risk of losing all hope for the future of her marriage. Neither she nor her husband lacked commitment to the relationship. They had no desire to separate, and their love for each other was unquestionably real. Yet neither of them was satisfied with the quality of their marital relationship. Things between them had been slightly off balance for years and there was no hint that improvement would be coming anytime soon.

Laura came to talk with us about her marital struggles. She did not come to us asking for our wise human counsel, but seeking divine revelation along with us. Only the supernatural wisdom of a holy God can provide solutions to seemingly insurmountable problems. The received presence of the Holy Spirit in even one partner gives the marital union access to the miraculous assets of God's kingdom of light. Supported by the glory of the Lord, the improbable becomes probable and the impossible becomes possible.

There are many people like Laura, both male and female, who experience an uncomfortable disconnect with their spouses over spiritual matters. The degree of separation caused by this is varied, but it is always painfully significant. Even when both partners are solidly committed to God, satan uses spiritual division as a weapon to attack individual relationships with God and undermine the stability of the marriage covenant itself. If this assault is not countered with the truth, love, and power of God, the results can be devastating.

We honor the Lauras of the world who demonstrate courage, integrity, and strength of commitment by staying the course, though unequally yoked in their marriages. Often it appears easier to simply leave, but they continue in relationship with their partners because of their desire to honor God. Hope seems barely real at times, yet it remains because they believe in God's unchanging truth and the goodness of His plan. They don't give up because they know "with God all things are possible" (Matthew 19:26).

If you are in the same situation as Laura, please allow us to share a few practical tips concerning the struggles of your marriage. God joyfully shares His wisdom and knowledge with those who desire to learn. Through God's wisdom and knowledge being communicated, He will prosper both you and your marital union. You will be blessed when you find wisdom and gain understanding, for these are more profitable than silver and yield better returns than gold (Proverbs 3:13–14). Through knowledge your life will be "filled with rare and beautiful treasures" (Proverbs 24:4). Because you have tasted the sweet goodness of God, there is "a future hope for you, and your hope will not be cut off" (Proverbs 24:14).

For the Lord gives wisdom, and from his mouth come knowledge and understanding. He holds victory in store for the upright, he is a shield to those whose walk is blameless, for he guards the course of the just and protects the way of his faithful ones. (Proverbs 2:6–8)

Practical Tips

Following are a few of the things God brought to our minds the night we talked and prayed with Laura:

- Just like you, your spouse was created in God's image. There are abilities and attributes placed in him or her that are part of God's sovereign will. These things are worthy of respect. So honor your spouse whenever this is appropriate.
- Let the peace of Christ rule in your heart and be thankful (Colossians 3:15). Honestly express thankfulness whenever possible for your spouse and for the things he or she does.
- God has a wonderful plan for you, and He has a specific and amazing plan for your marital partner as well.
- Jesus loved your spouse enough to die for him or her.
- You can learn to supernaturally love *(agape)* your mate even if this kind of love does not seem to be deserved in the natural realm. Jesus said we are to even love our enemies (Matthew 5:44).
- Your loving behavior must not be dependent on your partner's response. Jesus loved us first while we were totally undeserving. He died for us knowing we would

behave in ungodly ways (Romans 5:6). "We love because he first loved us" (1 John 4:19).

- The kind of love God requires cannot come from within you or be manufactured by your will. Ask for divine revelation as to how to love your spouse. Supernatural love for another person is not based on who he or she is now. It is enabled by prophetically visualizing who that person was created to be.

- Accept and obey creative instructions from the Holy Spirit as to how to show love to your partner. Do not reject anything you are told to do by the Spirit of God. The ways of God often do not make sense to our natural minds, but when we are obedient, they always produce wonderful results.

- Do not compromise by accepting a mediocre result. Continue to pursue every aspect of supernatural marriage available to you and your spouse.

- Do not be discouraged by your present circumstances. Where you are today does not limit where God can take you in the future.

- Miraculous transformation can happen in a moment. So be expecting the impossible to happen at any time.

- Hope will not disappoint you (Romans 5:5). God placed hope in your heart to give you the joy, strength, and faithfulness that bridge across satan's trap of discouragement. Do not underestimate the significance of your role in completing God's plan. The fulfillment of hope is catalyzed by the supernatural love of God flowing through you. This unstoppable love will bless you and your entire household.

- Do not place blame on the spouse to whom you are unequally yoked. Blame will breed bitterness and resentment. This further injures a relationship instead of fostering healing.

- There is never an acceptable excuse for words or actions intended to cause pain. Inappropriate things said or done by your partner do not justify retaliation. We are instructed to bless even those who persecute us: "Bless those who persecute you; bless and do not curse" (Romans 12:14).

- Second Timothy 2:23–24 instructs us, "Don't have anything to do with foolish and stupid arguments, because you know they produce quarrels. And the Lord's servant must not quarrel; instead, he must be kind to everyone." *Everyone* includes your marital partner. Arguments cannot continue if the fruit of the Spirit is supernaturally present in your heart and mind, and expressed in your words. Ask God for more of the fruit of the Spirit to be produced and evident in your life.

- Avoid dwelling on critical thoughts of your spouse. Take every thought captive to obey Christ (2 Corinthians 10:5). "Whatever is noble" and "whatever is admirable … think about such things" (Philippians 4:8).

- How big is your God? Giving up hope indicates a belief that your marital relationship is too crippled for even God to heal. Do you really believe His promises? Trust that God will provide everything you need to live out your life (2 Peter 1:3).

- Earnestly ask God for help. Then do everything He shows you to do with the wisdom, patience, kindness, and goodness He supplies. Consistently demonstrate all fruit of the Spirit. This is not only your job description; it is who you are meant to be.

- Regardless of your partner's responses, righteous living is not in vain. Godly behavior will store up treasures in heaven for you (Matthew 6:20) and can sanctify an unbelieving spouse (1 Corinthians 7:14).

- Jesus came that you could have life to the full (John 10:10). Abundant life in you attracts your spouse to the Source of life.

Key to Abundant Life

The key to abundant life is true intimacy with God. The more deeply you are in love with Him, the more genuinely you can love your spouse. God's perfect love is ultimately the source of everything required to create and sustain supernatural marriage. You must not lose hope, because nothing can separate you from this everlasting love (Romans 8:35). Ultimately, His love is all you need.

Your desire for supernatural marriage is not a selfish wish. It is a spiritual recognition of how things should be. You may be confident His plan for you is completely good (Jeremiah 29:11). God's Word is truth (John 17:17) and every one of His promises will be fulfilled (Joshua 23:14).

We pray that you will be blessed as you read the words of this passage from Isaiah 61. God wrote them for you. Indeed, they were written about you.

> The Spirit of the Sovereign LORD is on me, because the LORD has anointed me to preach good news to the poor. He has sent me to bind up the brokenhearted, to proclaim freedom for the captives and release from darkness for the prisoners, to proclaim the year of the LORD's favor and the day of vengeance of our God, to comfort all who mourn, and provide for those who grieve in Zion—to bestow on them a crown of beauty instead of ashes, the oil of gladness instead of mourning, and a garment of praise instead of a spirit of despair. They will be called oaks of righteousness, a planting of the LORD for the display of his splendor.
>
> They will rebuild the ancient ruins and restore the places long devastated; they will renew the ruined cities that have been devastated for generations. Aliens will shepherd your flocks; foreigners will work your fields and vineyards. And you will be called priests of the LORD, you will be named ministers of our God. You will feed on the wealth of nations, and in their riches you will boast.

Instead of their shame my people will receive a double portion, and instead of disgrace they will rejoice in their inheritance; and so they will inherit a double portion in their land, and everlasting joy will be theirs. (Isaiah 61:1–7)

ABOUT THE AUTHORS

Dr. Dan and Linda Wilson are marriage missionaries. They delight in traveling around the world blessing marriages and sharing about Jesus. Taking the call to support widows and children seriously, they are involved with multiple orphanages and mission projects in several nations. Dan and Linda are cofounders of Supernatural Marriage and Missions, created to encourage Spirit-led intimacy in marriages through conferences, teaching, writing, and personal counseling. They have two sons enjoying their own supernatural marriages and four beautiful grandchildren. The Wilsons reside in Fort Worth, Texas.

Dan and Linda Wilson appreciate receiving any comments you might have about *7 Secrets of a Supernatural Marriage* or their ministry. They are not able to provide personal counsel via e-mail. However, you can contact them via their website at SupernaturalMarriage.org.

For more information concerning supernatural marriage and missions, to order more copies of this book, or for information about attending or hosting a Supernatural Marriage event, please visit SupernaturalMarriage.org.

**Other Books by Dr. Dan and Linda Wilson
available at SupernaturalMarriage.com**

Lovemaking (coming in 2015)

CO-: Powerful Partners in Marriage

Experiencing Supernatural Marriage: A Study Guide

Supernatural Marriage: The Joy of Spirit-Led Intimacy
(available in Spanish and Finnish translations)